Break-up
Breakthrough

A 37-DAY GUIDE FROM
HEARTBREAK TO HEALING

DEDICATION

A 37-Day Guide from Heartbreak to Healing is dedicated to my mother, Ludie Hodges; my sisters, Ernestine Harris, Johnnie Hodges and Shirley Todd; and all the other women who poured into me, teaching me their secrets.

INTRODUCTION

Ending a relationship can be one of the most painful and emotional occurrence that a person will ever experience. It can also be cathartic, liberating and transformative, depending on the individual's attitude and quest for self-knowledge and discovery.

During a difficult break-up, a person's mind and soul are usually open and raw. That state of openness presents a perfect opportunity to stop, listen and learn about the decisions, personal history and patterns that formed the backdrop for the relationship, as well as its demise.

For most people, a break-up is a time when they will be vulnerable, introspective and in search of solutions and remedies to stop their pain. During a break-up, they are more willing to examine their behaviors and choices. This willingness can produce a reflectiveness that can open their minds and important relationship lessons can be learned.

Many relationship pitfalls can be revealed and many previous choices will be clearer at this time. If the insights and lessons learned through the break-up are heeded, a break-up can be a life changing breakthrough that can change a person's momentum and trajectory. It can also provide an opportunity to critically and logically examine what went wrong and how to make personal adjustments, which will better prepare him or her for the next relationship, helping to avoid the pitfalls from the last.

This break-up analysis will shed light on your relationship patterns and how you may have given yourself away too cheaply. It can reveal who you are in relationships and what you need to do to get back on the right track in order to find a nurturing and fulfilling love that's good to you and good for you.

3

If you are looking for tips to get your lover back, this is the wrong book for you. A large majority of the relationships that people fight to hold on to are toxic and dysfunctional, but because some people are fearful of their future relationship prospects, they hold on to a relationship that's hurting them mentally, emotionally and sometimes even physically.

For their own personal growth and relationship health, it would make more sense for them to run hollering and screaming from these toxic relationships rather than trying to hold on to them. For this reason, there will not be any advice on how to wear your hair different, perform sexual acts more proficiently, lose ten pounds quickly nor will there be a conversations about games to play to make your partner miss you. Wrong Book!

The intention of this book is to help you find the loving relationship that you deserve. _Break-up Breakthrough_ assumes from the outset that the relationship, for whatever reason, is over and that the reader is attempting to heal, transform and make better relationship decisions in the future.

Break-up Breakthrough was designed to give you the tools to use your break-up as the impetus to transform your life and position yourself to attract the love that you need by honestly looking at yourself and what you contributed to the relationship's dysfunction. Additionally, it will help you analyze the past and point you toward the promise of a better future.

The starting point of this 37-day process assumes that you are aware that your relationships have not been healthy or fulfilling and that you want to be different; to love differently and to be loved differently. If you want a different kind of relationship because your previous relationships have left you feeling used and abused, you are in a perpetual state of heartbreak or you are wondering why your relationships seem to always fall apart, you will find questions and answers, solace and hope in these pages.

4

If you follow the steps outlined in _Break-up Breakthrough_, you will acquire the tools necessary to help repair your broken places and attract a person who will appreciate your uniqueness and nurture your spirit. Break-up Breakthrough provides the questions that you need to answer to understand your relationship patterns and personal history. It requires you to engage in honest and truthful self-assessment in order to glean the insights you need.

Answers are not provided because the answers, insights, and transformation come from your ability to be honest with yourself and tell your own personal truth. The questions, exercises and homework are guides that will assist you in your transformation. However, the transformation is in direct correlation with your efforts, honesty, willingness to heal and your commitment to learning the lessons you need for your soul to soar. If you are ready to work and grow, then you've stopped at the right place and I applaud you for your decision.

This book will guide you over the next 37 days (more if you need it), to look at yourself, your relationship patterns, how those patterns came to be, and how they have influenced your relationship choices. Break-up Breakthrough allows you to work at your own pace. Some days the work will be easy and other days you may unearth a difficult revelation that might require you to take some time to process. Take your time to understand your feelings and appreciate the information they may provide. Remember to be kind to yourself. Don't absorb blame for not knowing what you didn't know and don't take credit for the bad behavior of others.

When you have completed this program, you will have learned to make better relationship decisions in addition to transforming your awareness of your relationship patterns and personal history. Doing this will help you to be your best you and attract the love that you want and need. We will have some fun along the way; we will laugh and we will cry. But in the end you will become VERY clear on the difference between what you want and what you need; you will understand what will drain your spirit and what will replenish it.

5

MY STORY

It a is very difficult task to talk about the pain of a break-up, if you've ever been through one. As children, we all have our little crushes that don't pan out and our feelings get hurt. We sulk and our mothers come to the rescue, tell us how great we are and give us our favorite treat. Somehow we know that we'll survive and once again all is good with the world.

Those little disappointments are expected, however, when you're an adult and you've given your life and poured your whole being into a relationship, only to have it come tumbling down on you, that's a different story. It feels as if the world will never be the same again.

There are usually signs that something is off, but most of the time we don't see them. Then when the relationship collapses it catches us completely by surprise. The pain of a fresh heartbreak is almost unbearable; no words can really describe it. You physically hurt but you're not exactly sure where the pain is coming from. You wonder if the pain is actually coming from your heart, your brain or from deep within every tissue and fiber of your body.

I didn't know where the pain was truly coming from, all I knew was that I wanted it to stop! I willed it to stop but it didn't. I knew I had to make it stop and I wanted to make sure that it never happened to me again. I couldn't talk to anyone about it because I thought of myself as a strong woman, yet I was reduced to rubble and I was hurt and embarrassed. The last thing I wanted was for him to find out how devastated I really was, so I pretended all was well and his leaving had no effect on me. All the while, I felt like I was dying inside and all I wanted to do was run away from it all; but I had to wake up every day and face the world.

6

Even though I was cautious in the beginning, he was still able to break down all of my walls and for the first time, I truly gave myself, all of me. I laid my soul open. There was nothing I wouldn't have done for him and I honestly thought the feeling was mutual.

You see, I had always been a very reserved person. I was a mathematician, logical and scientific. I'd looked at people acting foolishly in love and thought to myself, "this doesn't make sense!" I had never experienced that type of love or the resulting heartbreak. I watched my friends and family members as they made tragic relationship mistakes because they were "in love" and thought" that's a crock!" Not me, I wanted to be totally self-sufficient and never want or need anything or anyone. But he came along and something was different, he understood me, never pressured me, respected me and he LOVED me!

Then after five years, he LEFT and I was completely devastated. In fact devastated isn't a strong enough word, neither is annihilated or destroyed. I cried so many tears I wondered where my body was getting the water to continue producing more, but the tears continued to flow.

I didn't know what to do with myself. I was acting foolishly in love. The 'crock' was real. I took pain relievers but they had no effect on the type of pain I was feeling. The only time I had ever felt even remotely like this was when there was a death in my family.

I was lost. I didn't know what to do and I was tired of feeling sick. So I crawled up in my bed with a legal pad and tried to journal the pain away. I thought if I could get my pain out on paper it would be something tangible that I could hold in my hand and then just discard. It didn't work! I knew if I was going to survive, I needed a plan and it was going to have to come from within me.

I gave myself thirty days to learn a new lesson, skill or insight that would make my plight easier. I wanted to learn anything that would help me process what I was feeling.

7

I drew upon my counseling and mathematical background and it took everything I had inside of me to draw up a plan. I called it my "How to get over HIM plan". Later I named it *Break-up Breakthrough.*

I'm sharing my plan with the hope and prayer that it will also help you to survive the loss of your love. I created it because I was too ashamed, embarrassed and stubborn to ask for help or even let anyone see my pain. I didn't have a guide or a resource to advise me, so I wrote one for my own survival. I needed to survive the loss of a love that was still walking around.

Today, my survival guide is 37 days in duration, because I learned more lessons in the process that I think would be valuable to your recovery. Break-up Breakthrough, a 37 day guide from Heartbreak to Healing helped me get through a very painful period and I came out on the other side with more clarity and understanding.

Some daily assignments took me three or four days to complete, but slowly I began to feel a new normal taking shape. I emerged from my nightmare a little better, a little stronger and much wiser every day, and it was painful to admit that it wasn't all him. I found that I had played a significant role in my own heartbreak.

I tucked my plan away until a close friend went through something similar. I went to her so she would not be alone. I cried with her because I knew her pain. I shared the plan with her and we worked through it together every day and she told me how the process really helped her to see her life more clearly. We tucked the tear stained pages away again, until another one of our friends went through a divorce. I knew my plan had value and I'd share various lessons with people I knew, but the plan was just a document tucked away in a bottom drawer until the next opportunity came around to use it again.

Then one day I saw Halle Berry on the Oprah show talking about her failed marriage to Eric Benet and I thought, "I wish I could share my plan with her." She was smiling as she talked but I knew her pain and

and what it was like to have to hold yourself together when it felt like your heart had been smashed into too many pieces to count.

I've always admired Halle. She is beautiful and seems to have a kind and loving Spirit, but she appears to be very unlucky in love. I prayed for her and didn't think of it again. But when I read about her next failed relationship I thought, "Maybe, I should share my Break-up Breakthrough survival guide with the world." After all, most people go through at least one horrible break-up in a lifetime and maybe my hard learned lessons would make their experience easier to endure.

Over the years, I've learned that people have different ways of coping with heartbreak. Some close themselves down to love forever, never giving themselves to love again, never trusting their ability to love or be loved. That's such a tragedy, because even though closing down keeps you from getting hurt, it also keeps you from the love that's standing just outside of your walls. Oftentimes the separation can be just as painful as the heartbreak. People don't realize that it's much better to learn a few techniques to protect their hearts as they attempt to give themselves in love to a deserving partner. Closing down and hiding from love only creates another set of emotional dilemmas and issues.

Other broken-hearted lovers will turn their heartbreak into permission to break the hearts of others in an attempt to get even with their past partners. But even with the pain they inflict on others they are never whole again. Furthermore, the world is robbed of more love and hearts free to be who they were created to be. This cycle of pain keeps on going and healing is denied because the wounded will not admit that they are just hurt individuals trying to hurt others to keep from feeling their own pain.

Even still, other broken-hearted lovers will keep making the same mistakes over and over. They don't understand how their patterns and their past continue to lead them to the same places. They begin to think they are flawed people not deserving of love rather than realizing that they merely have a few roadblocks that need to be cleared in order to make better relationship decisions. These roadblocks continue to fulfill their deepest relationship fears, and the cycle continues, turning their love lives into a self-fulfilling prophecy of one heartbreak after another.

Lastly, there are some of us who learn from our failed relationships and heartbreaks. We feel the same pain but we know that there's hope. We vow to love again and to be smarter about who we chose to give our hearts to. We embrace our heartbreak, soothe it, learn from it, open our hearts and give love another try.

Please know that we are creatures created by God to love and be loved. Sometimes the love we seek is difficult, short lived and tainted, but we cannot give up on the possibility that true love will find us. Remind yourself that holding back from love keeps you protected from hurt but absent from the love that wants to embrace you. I hope and pray that you will choose to learn from your heartbreak and use these daily lessons, exercises, observations and questions as balm to help take the soreness and pain away.

I sincerely hope that somewhere in these pages you will find healing, understanding and the courage to love again. I hope you will recognize your patterns and address them, but most of all I pray you will find the love a heart like yours deserves. I pray that you find a partner who will hold your heart as their greatest treasure.

Blessings.

DAY 1
It's Your Party, Cry if You Want To

So many times we have been taught to pretend that we are okay when we are not.

- Big boys/girls don't cry.
- Never let them see you sweat.
- Don't get mad, get even.

These lessons have their place, but sometimes learning them too well helps you push your emotions down and lose yourself to the bravado. When this happens, you pretend so much that you lose track of your authentic self and true emotions become frightening and paralyzing. In reality, when you're in pain, it will best benefit you to take the time to clear that energy, feel the pain and loss, grieve it, learn from it and move on. If you continually pretend that you're not in pain and that the grief isn't there, you prolong the agony of the break-up and delay your breakthrough.

The biggest mistake that you can make is to push your pain away and pretend it does not exist. People who try to pretend they are not hurting usually rush into another relationship with the unfinished business from the last one. When this happens, all of this residual toxic energy builds up and begins to work on your psyche and you begin to doubt your self-worth, and whether or not you are worthy of being loved. Those doubts lead to personal turmoil and more poor relationship choices.

Expressing your grief is very important. If you don't express it, it will build up and either explode into destructive behaviors or implode leaving you in a state of depression and despair. Neither option is good. Some destructive results of unexpressed grief are:

11

- Empty or Dysfunctional Relationships
- Drugs/Alcohol use
- Self-Defeating Patterns
- Risky Behaviors
- Eating Disorders
- Poor Self Esteem
- Depression and Isolation

All of these things can happen just because you're sad and you want to pretend that things are okay when they're not. Grief is personal. Everyone feels it differently, expresses it differently and gets over it at different times. Sometimes people never recover from grief. It can eat away at a person until they become disconnected, angry and depressed people who spew negatively at everyone they come into contact with.

Today, Day One of your 37 day _Break-up Breakthrough_ Challenge, your assignment, and I hope you accept it, is to give yourself permission to cry if you need to. Today, give yourself permission to stop being strong and feel what's really in your heart. You don't have to pretend that you feel fine when you're hurting.

It's a very important skill to know when you need a tourniquet. In order to grasp your healing and transformation, you must get in touch with the feelings you may have stuffed down and hidden from the world. It's important to be in touch with your emotions, to acknowledge them, feel them and release them. Tell yourself the truth, be vulnerable to your feelings and refuse to suppress what you've endured and how you honestly feel.

While in graduate school I had to study the stages of grief. One of the things I learned is that the level of stress associated with a bad break-up or divorce can be in the same clinical range as the stress caused by an actual death. They both need to be grieved and grief is a process.

Take time to grieve and depending on how long the relationship lasted and how deeply you felt, you might need to take more than one day on today's challenge. However, PLEASE don't spend more than three days on this step, because it's easy to become addicted to the sadness and go into a depressed state, where you tell everyone who will listen how you have been victimized.

Try not to draw others into your misery. You don't need company, you need healing. The key is to give yourself permission to really feel and to even fall apart if you need to. Feel the loss. Learn from it. See the associated patterns and decide to move on. Then prepare for your breakthrough.

If you have kids, it will be difficult for them to see mommy or daddy fall apart. So if you have the luxury of having someone keep the kids for you, please do that. If not, find a space and time where you can give yourself permission to expel the toxic energy, sadness and grief that comes along with a relationship break-up. Sometimes, the emotions are bottled up because you have to be strong for others and you think you can't give yourself time to process your emotions. Give up the brave face, momentarily.

Sometimes it's good to let your children and others see portions of your grief and pain. It may in return give them permission to feel what they feel. But, please know that if you don't find the time, the grief you feel will come out at inopportune times or in destructive behaviors.

Sometimes people focus on who will fill the empty space that has been vacated rather than learning from the break-up and transforming their life because of it. When the focus is on finding a replacement relationship, rather than healing yourself and learning the lessons associated, it usually ends with another break-up because the relationship started for the wrong reasons. It started from a place of neediness and despair rather than a space of health and sincerity. Give yourself permission. If you journal, please get all your emotions out on paper. If you don't journal, talk to a tape recorder,

13

draw a picture, use a punching bag, run five miles, just get it out. Release it and clear a space for you to learn, grow and transform.

So, please remember today to give yourself time to grieve. It's your party, cry if you want (or need) to.

See you tomorrow.

14

DAY 2
ACT OUT-- GET EVEN

Were you betrayed? Lied to? Taken advantage of? Abused? Deceived? Conned? Left in financial ruin? LET'S REALLY GET EVEN! And then let's be better.

Today is an imaginary day! I want you to think of all the mean and nasty things you would like to do to get even. Indulge yourself with thoughts of what you should say, what you wanted to say, and what you would say if given the opportunity. What mean awful things would you do? Think about them, bring them to the surface and enjoy them for a few minutes. However, before you make any phone calls, write any letters, post anything online, rant on Facebook or twitter, slash any tires or break the window out of cars, remind yourself that there are consequences to each action. Release all this negative energy and prepare for your breakthrough. There are three words that you should always consider before you perform any action, especially a negative one. These words are:

karma
Karma
KARMA

After you have thought about the mean and awful things, decide to be a different person. A BETTER person. Decide to be the person that you would want to be with. Release the negative energy and realize that the best revenge is to become the best YOU and to find a fulfilling long-term relationship that provides the bliss that is your birthright.

Acting out or trying to get even could tarnish your reputation, get you arrested, shame your family and a myriad of other bad consequences that you will regret.

15

If you let it go, karma has a way of working things out. Think about it as if you were in school. If you goof off in class, the consequence is a failing grade, but if you pay attention to each lesson, study, ask for help when you need it, the consequence is a passing grade that allows you to move on to the next grade and continue learning. The same concept can be applied to relationships: listen, learn, analyze and transform. If you do learn from the relationship, you will better understand how to weed out bad relationships before they go too far and save yourself from repeating the same mistakes again.

With the tools and questions that you learn during this 37-day challenge, you will be able to look back at past relationships and see where they went wrong. Once you recognize your patterns and motivations, you will have a 100-watt light bulb moment.

Make a conscious decision to be better, do better, and show all who are watching that you have class and style. No matter how badly you were treated, the goal is to learn the lesson from the relationship, heal yourself and move on to bigger and better love. Don't linger in the negativity; release the negative energy associated with this relationship and formulate a new agenda for your life and future relationships. If you don't learn the lesson now, you will have to learn it in the next relationship or the next. Therefore, it's best to learn it now!!! Make an uncompromisable decision to be a better person and place your energy on what benefits you rather than what hurts you.

I believe strongly that what you do comes back to you, so you have to set your life up to receive good things. Some call it the law of attraction, which says you will attract what you focus on. If you allow yourself to do vile, evil things to others, the negative energy will come back to you. It might take awhile but it will always come back to you. Trying to get even with your ex brings your energy down and can likely land you in jail or a state of embarrassment that can affect not only you but also all the people who love you.

So for today, the assignment is to release the negativity, clear your energy and decide to focus on your healing, as well as position yourself for the breakthrough that has your name on it.

16

Besides, you don't want to give your ex the satisfaction of knowing that you fell completely apart and stooped to such low levels. You are better than that. You have more class and self-respect than to go off the deep end and act irresponsibly.

If you let it go, karma has a way of working things out. Think about it as if you were in school. If you goof off in class, the consequence is a failing grade, but if you pay attention to each lesson, study, ask for help when you need it, the consequence is a passing grade that allows you to move on to the next grade and continue learning. The same concept can be applied to relationships: listen, learn, analyze and transform. If you do learn from the relationship, you will better understand how to weed out bad relationships before they go too far and save yourself from repeating the same mistakes again.

With the tools and questions that you learn during this 37-day challenge, you will be able to look back at past relationships and see where they went wrong. Once you recognize your patterns and motivations, you will have a 100-watt light bulb moment.

Make a conscious decision to be better, do better, and show all who are watching that you have class and style. No matter how badly you were treated, the goal is to learn the lesson from the relationship, heal yourself and move on to bigger and better love. Don't linger in the negativity; release the negative energy associated with this relationship and formulate a new agenda for your life and future relationships. If you don't learn the lesson now, you will have to learn it in the next relationship or the next. Therefore, it's best to learn it now!!! Make an uncompromisable decision to be a better person and place your energy on what benefits you rather than what hurts you.

I believe strongly that what you do comes back to you, so you have to set your life up to receive good things. Some call it the law of attraction, which says you will attract what you focus on. If you allow yourself to do vile, evil things to others, the negative energy will come back to you. It might take awhile but it will always come back to you.

Trying to get even with your ex brings your energy down and can likely land you in jail or a state of embarrassment that can affect not only you but also all the people who love you.

So for today, the assignment is to release the negativity, clear your energy and decide to focus on your healing, as well as position yourself for the breakthrough that has your name on it.

DAY 3

Resign Yourself (Face the Facts)
Don't play 20 Questions

Oftentimes when relationships fall apart we want to blame something or someone. We want to play the last conversations over and over in our heads like a news feed, trying to figure out the "if", "why", "how." Playing 20 Questions is an effort in futility. What if you did lose ten pounds? What if you did have more sex? What if you were more patient? What if you had done everything right? What if you had been a mind reader and knew your partner's innermost thoughts? What if? What if? What if?

The reality is that you can't change the past and you shouldn't let the past control you or your future. You have to release it and move on. The more prudent use of your time is to acknowledge where you are now and make every effort to understand your patterns of behavior, how you choose partners, what effect your childhood and family has on those decisions and how to make conscious decisions that will get you what you want.

You have to embrace the place where you are and learn the lessons, sooner rather than later. If you attempt to be who your partner wants you to be rather than your authentic self, you are compromising yourself. If you attempt to be someone else, keeping up the facade will continue to make you feel minimized, anxious, unsure and scared that you will be discovered.

Admit the relationship failed. Failed relationships happen to everyone, no matter who you are, no matter how pretty you are, how much you weigh, how smart you are or how much money you have in your bank account.

Relationships fail! We have all seen men and women who are beautiful, thin, glamorous, talented, rich and smart and they still have failed relationships; Halle Berry, Jennifer Aniston, Dennis Quaid, Robert Pattinson, Usher, Rihanna, just to name a few. All these people are altogether lovely, yet they have had relationship woes, so you're in good company.

Your breakthrough will come much faster if you face the fact that the relationship is over. It has run its course. It's over! It's time to remove it from life support and say your goodbyes. Hopefully you have some good memories and life changing insights that will make it worth the time and effort. Today, it's time to embrace the lesson from it so you can look closely at yourself and your patterns, and work on becoming the best version of you.

A good way to put this relationship into perspective is to remember the relationships where you have hurt someone and left that person wondering what was wrong with him or her and how they could make you love them. The reality of the matter was that loving them was just not something you could force your heart to do, even if you wanted to. Something happened or did not happen and the passion for that person was just not there. It didn't make them bad or flawed, you just didn't love them. You probably tried and maybe even faked it, but after awhile you had to admit to yourself that you were living a lie and it was unfair to continue to prolong that person's pain.

It's a painful situation no matter what side of the equation you're on. That's why it's important to embrace the hurt you've caused and the hurt you've endured, both will serve you well. If you learn the lessons from both situations, release the energy, grieve the loss, and vow to love again, then the process will be much easier.

One of my favorite songs is by a wonderful vocalist and former Broadway performer, Heather Headley. The lyrics are,

"I wish I could go back to the day before we met and skip my regret. I wish I was not in love with you then you couldn't hurt me."

If we, in our humanity had the ability to go back into our past and speak to ourselves before we made foolish mistakes, what a wonderful world that would be. It would be a great power to have. With that ability, we could have perfect lives and never have heartbreak, disappointments and brokenness. It's so very unfortunate that we don't have that power and we have to deal with the reality of the messes we make in our lives and the lives of others.

It's time out for pretending. A reality check is in order. Otherwise, in six months, two years or five years from now you will find yourself in the same broken-hearted situation yet again. Today, take the time to admit where you are, the decisions you made to get there and how you are going to learn from this place, this time and these feelings. You can no longer pretend that up is down and east is west. The place where your feet rest is a divine and holy place of instruction and transformation.

If you will stop today and learn what you think you already know; then the messages will become clearer and you can get in touch with the real you that you may have been trying to hide from. No diet plan, Botox, breast, butt or penile implants are going to make someone love you if they don't. "If I could just . . .!" isn't the question you should be asking; the correct question should be "How can I be a better person as a result of this relationship and its demise?"

The fact of the matter is that you have value just the way you are. Don't fool yourself into thinking that changing your hair color, bust size, weight or clothing will convince someone to love you when the simple fact is, they don't love you and that is a function of who they are and you cannot change their heart.

Embrace who you are, what you are and what you stand for, but resign yourself to grow, learn and improve yourself. Your focus should be on personal integrity, self-love and acceptance. Life will not be different until you choose to be different .

DAY 4
Confess --Analyze
THE 411

Today is a day for full transparency. It's time to admit to yourself the things you knew, but didn't want to admit that you knew. It's time to acknowledge the things that you wouldn't let yourself see or feel. The clues you failed to acknowledge and the information you pushed out of your mind.

Years ago, I discovered that you can usually learn most of the things you need to know about a person during the first couple of hours of conversation. You just need to know what questions to ask and how to listen. You don't listen for what he/she believes you want to hear, instead you listen for indications regarding their integrity, ideology about relationships, family history and individual character.

I would venture to guess that there were signs and clues that you overlooked in this most recent relationship and in past relationships. There were probably things you heard, saw or felt that you chose not to acknowledge or take into consideration. If you had consciously accepted those clues you would have had to make a conscious decision about the merits and viability of the relationship. So denying what you saw, heard or felt was much easier. If you didn't allow yourself to know what should have been clear, then you didn't have to admit that the relationship was flawed and dysfunctional. You chose to believe in the fairy tale that has now become this heart-breaking nightmare. Looking back in retrospect, *what were the clues you missed? What did you chose to ignore?*

A classic example of clues being ever present is a first date I had several years ago. My date and I met for dinner; the waitress was horrible. She was very inattentive and we had to ask someone to get her so we could order. Another waiter ended up bringing our food, some of which was cold.

Our drinks were never refilled and we asked several times for items we needed. I even had to get up and get my own silverware and refill our water glasses. The waitress was too busy flirting with three guys at another table to bother with us.

After trying to make the best of a bad restaurant experience, we asked and waited for our check. Fifteen minutes later, we were still waiting. My date tried to convince me to sneak out and not pay because we were being ignored and the food was not up to par. I agreed with his rationale and assessment of the situation but not his solution. I didn't want to get in trouble or go to jail for walking out without paying a $50.00 check.

Instead I called the manager and told him about our experience. The manager apologized profusely and comped the check and also gave us a gift card to come again. My date promptly took the gift card. My alarm bells went off immediately, was he selfish or just cheap? I kept quiet but I filed the information away in my "getting to know you file." He could have offered for us to use it but he simply took the card and put it in his wallet.

I went out with this guy a couple more times but I kept that incident in the back of my mind. It was clue number one. It seemed like a small thing, but it spoke to his selfishness and integrity. If a person doesn't have integrity in one aspect of their life, it will reveal itself in other aspects as well.

Clue number two was when he showed up at a social gathering and I knew he should have been at work. He said he had left work early and that a friend was covering for him. He seemed gleeful to tell me about an elaborate scheme that he and his friend used to cover for each other which allowed them to take off whenever they wanted to. Again, it spoke to his integrity, honesty and commitment.

There were a couple of other clues that reinforced my initial perception. I decided that this relationship would not suit my needs because

I saw his pattern of dishonesty, which would mean that I would never be able to fully trust him.

The question would always be in my mind, wondering what else he may be dishonest about. He made a good buddy to hang out with occasionally but there was no future for us as a couple.

Another example of overlooking the obvious came from a friend of mine. He married a woman who told him that she had never been faithful in a relationship. This should have been a major clue for him but he didn't receive it as such. They got married and he thought she would miraculously be faithful to him despite her track record. A couple of years into the marriage he discovered infidelity. I reminded him of the conversation he shared with me several years prior. He replied, "but she hadn't been married before." Marriage or not, there was a problem that he was aware of and he chose to ignore it. He didn't ask questions about how those relationship patterns would be addressed in the confines of their marriage. He assumed that just because they were married the cheating pattern would automatically dissipate.

Now the question is, what clues did you miss? What did you overlook? What was it that you just couldn't let yourself accept, embrace or acknowledge? Go back from the day you met and see things in retrospect. What clues were there all along? Look clearly, hear, see, feel and acknowledge what is before your eyes. Have you ever denied what you knew was the truth?

Your assignment for today is to think about this relationship and past relationships. List any clues you may have ignored or missed that would indicate that the relationship was doomed for failure.

DAY 5

Will the Real You Please Step Forward
I'd like to introduce . . .

The question I want you to consider today is who are you in your relationships? Are you a chameleon based on what relationship you're in? Do you reveal your "REAL" self? Did you do what you thought your partner wanted or did you present your true and authentic self? Yesterday, we tried to find out what clues you may have missed in discovering who your partner really was. Today we want to see if you played a part in the relationship deception, by not showing who you really are.

It's common in relationships to mold yourself to the person that you think your partner wants you to be. Sometimes it's basic relationship compromise that we all have to adhere to. If learning to put the toilet seat down is helping to make peace in your home, that's a basic relationship compromise. Also, if cleaning the make-up off the sink keeps him from going bonkers, that is also basic relationship compromise. However, when you make too many changes and concessions for the relationship, all evidence of your true self can be lost and people who know you may not even recognize you anymore; it becomes evident that your actions aren't normal relationship compromises. What part of you do you tend to give up in relationships?

- Are your wants, needs and desires replaced by your partners? If so, how does that usually manifest itself?
- Do you believe that you will not be loved if you are completely yourself?
- Did you feel minimized in this relationship?

When two people come together to form a relationship team or couple, there are always going to be some things that fall away as a result of the team becoming more important than each individual. However, when the things that fall away are very one-sided and one person feels overpowered by the other, then that becomes a problem.

When one personality is overshadowed and minimized by the other, the situation can easily become overbearing and abusive.

Individual habits should fall away because other things that are more important, desirable, and worthwhile take their place. Two individuals coming together to make a team have to find common ground and meet in the middle to produce a new normal. But when one partner pretends to be someone else to please the other partner it creates a hole in that person's self-esteem. When a person creates a relationship based character instead of being who they truly are, eventually the real personality will surface. Even the best actors in the world have to eventually come out of character.

So the question for today is "Who are you in your relationships?" Who do you become when you are coupled? What part of yourself do you tend to give up? Do you give up your friends? Do you lose you? Do you pretend to like baseball or musicals to please your partner, when you know you would rather watch paint dry than watch a baseball game or a musical? Have you faked being compatible with someone that you know you were not compatible with?

A healthy relationship promotes change and growth and there will be numerous situations where compromise is necessary. That is completely normal but when you give up your friends, hobbies, things you enjoy, your style, your dress, your hair color and your individuality, *you lose you.* This type of acting job will leave you drained, empty and alone.

However, if you present your whole self in your full glory and decide to be undeniably you, then you will tend to attract someone who wants you for you, loves you for you, is excited about the little quirks in your personality. And you will never have to worry about coming out of character.

I've heard some people say that you shouldn't show your true self until after you're married. I vehemently disagree with this, because no one likes to be bamboozled. No one likes to be deceived. What if your partner is in love with the carefully crafted facade rather than the true essence of who you are? A relationship or marriage built on lies and facades has no real foundation and it usually ends badly.

I know it sounds like something you learn in kindergarten or church school, but honesty really is the best policy in life and especially in relationships. Being honest gives you the right to also demand honesty. True self to true self is the desired and most meaningful combination. The story of my good friend is a great illustration of this. He was married for five years to a woman who he never saw without make-up. He never knew what her hair looked like without weave and during the divorce proceeding he discovered that he didn't even know how old she was. It was a relationship built on deception and doomed to fail.

You need to be who you are and make every attempt to make sure you know who you are involved with. Examine every clue; look at what's there instead of what you want to see. And most importantly make sure that you present your true self. Refrain from fragmenting yourself to maintain a relationship. If a fragmented self is necessary to maintain a relationship then that isn't a healthy relationship to be in. As my friend discovered with his wife, you can only fake it for so long and the truth will come out, believe me, the truth will come out.

Love yourself enough to find someone who supports you and accepts the real you. Don't lose who you are to maintain a relationship. You won't be happy if you can't be yourself. Present yourself boldly, unapologetically and be the real you, not some imitation of who someone wants you to be.

Your assignment for today is to list the ways you tend to compromise yourself in relationships.

DAY 6
The Teacher and the Lesson Plan

It was your decision to start this relationship. It was you that attracted him/her. It was you that made a decision to get involved. It was you that said yes to the relationship, because if this relationship was forced on you, then you probably wouldn't be sad that it is now over. It was you that taught him/her how to treat you. It was you, it really was, accept it and let's try to figure out what happened so you can release that pattern of behavior forever so that it doesn't plague any more of your relationships.

In relationships we usually choose people to help us with our unfinished patterns from the past. Little girls with daddy issues will usually chose a certain type of man. Children of abusive or alcoholic parents will usually chose a mate who is abusive or they will be abusive to a partner, even though it may takes months or even years for the characteristics to surface. Most of the time relationships are entered into without the conscious knowledge of these motivating factors. These subconscious blind spots keep you trying to work out family drama in your friendships and relationships. Some people never see the correlation between their relationships and their family patterns. By not learning this lesson, you continue the cycle of adding to your own suffering and creating more dysfunctional relationships.

You have to heal old scars from the past childhood trauma instead of constantly changing the bandages in the form of new dysfunctional relationships that lead to more and more heartbreak. At some point, you have to take off the bandages and clean the old wounds to prevent them from becoming infected again and again. If you don't clean these wounds, they will leave you feeling increasingly broken, damaged, and unlovable.

It might seem that talking about your family history has nothing to do

28

with your relationships, but there's no greater indication about how your relationships will turn out other than your family history. The hurts and heartaches from your childhood will inform and predict your adult relationship decisions.

In order to heal and transform your relationships, you have to first realize the impact that the past has had on your present relationships. If you don't become aware of the patterns that control your decision making, your early childhood issues will plague every aspect of your relationships. If you want things to be different then you must become aware of the damage and the aftereffects of your childhood dysfunction. After the realization has set in, then you must forgive your parents and yourself for not realizing how you were letting the past rule your present and future. When it comes to relationships you have to heal backward, from your childhood forward to reap the benefits in your future relationships.

Take the time to test the theory for yourself by answering the following questions:

- What were the major distasteful characteristics of this relation ship?
- How did he/she treat you?
- How did being with him/her make you feel about yourself?
- What was it about him/her that attracted you?
- Have you had these feelings before?
- Have you felt like this in any other relationship in your life?
- Was there something remotely familiar about the relationship?
- When have you felt emotionally similar?

Answer these questions honestly about your most recent relationship. Then answer the same questions about the relationship you were involved in before this one and the one before that and the one before that. Now, answer the same questions about your relationship with your mother and your father. Are there patterns emerging?

29

Sometimes we come to realize that we often date the same man/woman with a different name. The names are different, but they have many characteristics in common. The way they make you feel is very similar and who you become in the relationship is also very similar. It's the same relationship dynamics repeating themselves until you consciously change it. Each time we get a little smarter and the dynamics aren't as blatant, but the underlying emotions are still the same.

After you have had time to thoughtfully answer these questions, turn your attention to some even bigger questions: Where did these patterns begin? Who else makes you feel the way you did in this relationship? How can you fix it? The first step is to go back to where these patterns first emerged, analyze the source and vow to stop playing out family drama in your relationships.

Your assignment for today is to analyze what your romantic relationships have in common and how they compare to patterns you have seen in your family.

DAY 7
You AGAIN

As we discussed yesterday, most people have relationship patterns that usually can be traced back to childhood. We all have patterns. Some are healthy and move us in the direction of our own personal happiness and fulfillment, while other patterns are destructive and lead us toward despair, sadness and relationship dysfunction. These healthy and unhealthy habits influence the decisions we make in relationships. As a result, some of these habits must be changed if you want a more fulfilling relationship.

To gauge your patterns, a helpful question to ask yourself is "How did this relationship show me who I am?" Very few of us had perfect childhoods. There are always things to mend, repair and overcome. The goal of this day is become aware of these patterns and how they have affected you.

Yesterday, the goal was to begin to look at your relationships and patterns of being in those relationships. Today, we want to look at how your patterns from childhood patterns have affected you over the years in your personal and romantic relationships.

There are several questions that you will need to answer in order to fully understand the impact and implications these patterns have in your life.

- In relationships, what position do you adopt?
  - ✔ Are you always yourself?
  - ✔ Are you the perpetual victim?
  - ✔ Are you the one that closes down?
  - ✔ Are you the person who wants to control everything and everyone?
  - ✔ Who do you become when you are coupled?

31

✔ Are you secure, insecure, bold and daring or are you afraid to ask for what you want?
✔ Do you discard your friends and make your partner your whole life?

• Is heartbreak your perpetual friend?
  ✔ If yes, then what purpose does heartbreak serve in your life?
  ✔ Does it help support your feelings of failure or unworthiness?
  ✔ What does it do for you?

• Do you choose men/women who make you feel bad because deep down you really do feel like you are bad?

• Do you create problems where there are none in order to have something to complain about?
  ✔ Are you absolutely impossible to please?
  ✔ Are you looking for a reason to break-up with your partner, be cause you believe they're going to break up with you?
  ✔ Do you feel unworthy of love?

All these questions will provide insights on who you really are and what impact these patterns have had on your life and your relationships.

People attract people in their lives for specific purposes and one of the most important purposes is to show you who you are. A lady I worked with complained to me that all men were dogs and they couldn't be trusted. I expressed my disagreement knowing some wonderful faithful men. However, I wanted to understand her perspective. She was adamant about her desire to give up on men and relationships because, she believed all men were inherently evil. As we talked, I began to explore why "all men are dogs" in her mind.

She identified five major relationships in her life from the time she was age 15 to 40. She had two failed marriages and three relationships lasting more than two years.

She said she had loved all these men but they were lying cheaters. Two of them she knew she shouldn't have trusted, but she thought she could change these womanizing men into faithful loving husbands by her sheer love and devotion. She saw how these two men treated other women, but she thought she would be different.

Two of the remaining relationships started while the men were in relationships with other women. She said the fifth man was an all around great guy and she thought she had found the exception to the rule until she uncovered an affair he had with a colleague.

She played her victim role very well, even though she had evidence that four of the five men she had been involved with were not trustworthy. When asked if she was untrustworthy, she said she was always faithful, however she had already stated that two of the men she was involved with were in relationships when she got involved with them. One of her patterns was choosing men who were unfaithful. Where did the pattern come from?

When we talked about her childhood, the source of this pattern was evident. She came from a family where she was the product of an affair. Her father was married to someone else when she was born and stayed married to his wife until he passed away. She talked about missed birthdays, and her father's constant lying and the cheating that was a part of her family pattern.

Her mother married when she was eight and she said she considered the stepfather more her real father. He was always there, faithful and supportive. Yet she yearned for her real father and his acceptance. She didn't feel secure in her father's love and she never felt as good as his "real" kids. She tried everything to prove she was worthy of his love. She was an honor roll student, a track star, president of the student council and earned several scholarships to college. Everything she attempted was all with the intention of getting her father's attention and love.

It never worked, so she found her father in each and every major

33

relationship that she had. She recreated the pain that she felt in her childhood, rewriting the script in each relationship. While attempting to convert the untrustworthy to trustworthy, she continued trying to convince each man that she was worthy of his love, just as she had done with her father.

She isn't unique. We all have family patterns. Take the time to make an honest assessment of your familial patterns.

• Determine how these patterns reveal themselves in your relationships?
• How are your relationships similar to what you experienced as a child?
• How do you recreate your childhood scenario?
• How do you continue to date the same man/woman with a different name?

Each of us have relationship patterns that we need to explore. We need to make sure that we know why we attract who we attract and how to use our patterns to make better decisions.

34

DAY 8

May I Introduce…
Knowing you

It's important to know your patterns, where those patterns originated and how those patterns have affected the person you have become. It's most important, however to know yourself, your flaws, shortcomings and of course your strengths. Knowing these things will provide the framework for finding a relationship that's meaningful and real. The knowledge of your natural attraction patterns will help you better understand your relationship choices.

As we discussed, sometimes people are attracted to the things and people which allow them to play out past family drama. Everyone has baggage that they are carrying from childhood. It can only hurt you if it remains an unconscious pattern. When you become aware of this common pattern you can change it and stop casting your romantic interests into the roles that help you to work on your unfinished business from childhood. You can then choose a partner based on your adult needs rather than your childhood needs. When you meet someone, there are several questions you need to ask yourself:

- Am I replaying past drama with a new leading man/woman?
- What past hurt am I trying to heal from this relationship?
- Why am I attracted to this person?
- Is this the same person I have always dated?

The first thing that you need to acknowledge is that you are enough and worthy of love. So many times people choose bad relationships because they don't feel that they are worthy of good ones. They're afraid of putting their true vulnerable selves on display so they accept the unacceptable and yield to a series of unsupportive and unfulfilling relationships.Learning to put the past in perspective and not continue to live in the past can help you develop a fresh relationship perspective and strategy.

35

You have to decide to be different, choose different people and have a different type of relationship that can be fulfilling, supportive, nourishing and loving, because that's what you deserve. When you use your past as a measuring stick you can look in the face of the prototype person that you've been dating all your life and go the other way when they approach you. When you realize these dating patterns are in effect, you may realize that your insecurity may be choosing partners instead of your good logic self.

There's no way to predict the future, but I believe inherently that all of us get a feeling, an indication, or some sense of where a specific relationship might lead us. Some of us will see the signs and stop, others will proceed with caution, while others will throw caution to the wind and reserve our usual room in the Heartbreak Hotel.

A friend's daughter was a young pre-med student studying for entrance exams into medical school, when she met the local party guy who believed that "we were born to party" and nothing mattered but "the party". He made it clear to her that if she wanted to be with him, she needed to party with him. She knew instinctively that if she was not at the party he would probably hook-up with someone else.

On the other hand, she knew she needed to be studying but in order to be with him she sacrificed studying and started to party constantly. Any reasonable person would have known that there would be consequences to this decision and eventually a clash would erupt.

My first question would be, "does she have a pattern of self-sabotage?" Logically there was evidence that this might not have been the best coupling for her but she decided to throw caution to the wind and that single decision had the possibility of changing the course of her entire life.

Of course she could change her mind at any time and get back on track, but the bigger issue is why would anyone choose a relationship that would adversely affect his or her long and short-term goals?

36

Productive relationships add value to your life and support your goals, rather than limit your possibilities. I realize that this is an extreme example and most likely your issues may be a little subtler. However the point is there were indications of a bad coupling from the very beginning.

I'm sure that at some point in your life you have known someone who has made a similar relationship decision that changed the trajectory of his or her life. If this situation ever presents itself to you, it will be up to you to see the obstacles and contradictions and choose wisely, using your adult mind not your childhood patterns.

Adding value to your life is what a good relationship is supposed to do. Every relationship that comes into your life will leave a mark and change who you are because of the experience. Ask yourself how this relationship will leave you. Will it get you closer to your goals?

A healthy relationship will help you unearth hidden, submerged subconscious pain, confusion, despair, heartaches and feelings of unworthiness, and replace these feelings with joy, support and acceptance. You will be able to relax and rejoice in just being you because you will be able to stop the pretense and be your authentic self.

In a good relationship you can grow together, change and become better as a part of a couple rather than an individual. A healthy relationship can do these things because it provides a foundation of healthy coupling. You will have a soft place to fall when life gets difficult. You can stop hiding and be totally loved and accepted for who you are. A good relationship is chosen from a place of strength and awareness, rather than fear and old wounds.

What most people settle for isn't nearly what they want, need or deserve. They don't believe they deserve better, so they keep choosing mommies, daddies, their third grade teacher, an abuser, a bully or whoever was instrumental in helping to create the wounds in their souls. When you know why you chose what you chose, you can make a new and better decision. You can choose you.

37

Your assignment for today is make a list of the people you have dated and next to each name make a list of the things that attracted you to this person. What were the motivating factors in the relationship and how did they make you feel. As a result of the relationship, were you closer or further away from your goals? Be careful to note the emergence of any patterns.

DAY 9
What Next
The Order Form

Knowing that you teach people how to treat you is a lesson that's so very important. I pray that if you understand nothing else in these 37 days, it's that you teach people how to treat you by what you allow, accept and demand. Accept the responsibility of the teacher and decide how you want to be treated.

Any behavior that does not coincide with how you want to be treated needs to be examined, addressed and rectified. Every person should demand to be treated with dignity and respect. The only way to achieve this is to treat yourself in the manner that you want others to treat you. If you neglect yourself, others will neglect you. If you don't make yourself a priority in your own life, then no one else will make you a priority in their lives either. Treat others well, demand to be treated well and you will set the standard and advocate for yourself.

Always be mindful of how you are loving you. What loving things do you do to feed your body, mind and spirit? Treat your body right; make provisions for yourself the way you would for someone you love. If you take care of your body by feeding it regularly and healthily, people will notice. Also make an effort to refrain from consuming any-thing that does not promote life, health and longevity.

Take small steps and multiply them, even if it starts with loving your body enough to make yourself a good breakfast or choosing some clothes that fit your body correctly. When you look better, you also feel better and you have to feel good to attract good. Exercise to get the blood flowing and the toxins out of your body. Love your body the way you want a lover to; feed it, dress it, appreciate it, know it and listen to it to make sure it functions the way it should.

Your mind is a vital part of your overall being and it needs to be

39

nourished as well. Put some positive things in your mind like affirmations, self-help knowledge and current events. Look for positive things that make life exciting for you. Think good thoughts and always embrace any opportunity to learn something new. Be conscious of your thoughts and try to avoid negative self-talk. Your internal critic who reminds you of the past and is critical of your efforts is powerful, but it can be tamed. Become aware of and replace your negative thoughts with thoughts that support, appreciate and nourish you.

Additionally, your spirit will guide you if you get in touch with the love inside of you that is waiting to be expressed. Take some time to be quiet and listen to your inner self. I don't know what you believe or who you believe in, but whatever it is stop, listen and invite it to have a more expansive role in your development of a loving, more sensitive you.

Loving yourself through your past mistakes and not beating yourself up is crucial. Learning to order up what you want is also very important. When looking for a new mate, learn to make a new order form and if you happen to get something that doesn't fit, know you can change your mind. You can return it at any time. If your order isn't right, send it back.

I've seen many frustrated and angry men and women who are feeling the negativity because they simply give too much and receive so little in return. They neglect themselves and wonder why others neglect them as well. There's more of a tendency for women to over extend themselves trying to make sure everything is done and everyone is happy, at the sacrifice of self. The time to correct this practice is at the beginning of a new relationship. Set a new agenda and demand to be supported and appreciated as a part of the relationship foundation. Make sure support and appreciation are near the top of your order form. Don't start the neglect pattern and you will not have to keep it.

In a healthy relationship both partners are important and neither should be sacrificed for the sake of the other. Don't be so desperate that you will take anything and everything. Remember to *"Start out the way you plan to finish!"*

This is one of the most valuable lessons my mother ever taught me. It's a simple concept and it simply means if you plan to be minimized, neglected, abused and starved for attention and affection, then accept that kind of treatment from the beginning. You are then training your partner to treat you poorly and take you for granted. This is what you will endure during the duration of the relationship. Your partner will know that his/her actions hurt you, but also that you will always come back for more abuse, because you taught them that it was acceptable to treat you this way. If you start out this way, that's what you will get for years to come and it will have come from your own training.

Create a new normal for your life. The past is the past and you can't change it, but you can order up something new and different. Think about all the good guys/girls you may have overlooked or discounted and vow not to do it anymore. Look at the spirit of a person and who will be best suited for your long-term goals. Don't judge others too harshly. If you meet someone who is wonderful but has a few extra pounds don't automatically discount them. See if they have a loving heart. Maybe they will make you laugh and feel free. Take the time to think it through logically before placing them in the friend zone. I don't minimize the need for physical attraction; however it should be on the list but not the complete list.

Start off by being completely you. If you start a new relationship off by not speaking the truth, giving everything and expecting nothing, then most likely that's the way it will end. If you know you don't like going to every high school football game in the city, then respectfully decline, tell the truth and agree to go to some if it's that important to your partner. Otherwise, let that person find someone who enjoys what they enjoy if it is not acceptable for you.

Be honest, state your truth and live by it. Learn from the past, chose to be your wonderful, glorious self and know that you are good enough and you don't have to hide behind a façade. Step out and be unapologetically you. It's time to establish new relationship habits that will nourish you.

41

Develop habits that you can live with and rely on for the next twenty, thirty or forty years. You can decide to implement change in your life whenever you are ready.

Your assignment for today is to complete your order form. What do you need to be happy? What kind of relationship do you need?

DAY 10
Changing Expectations
The What, When and Why?

Each person that comes into your life comes for a reason, a season or a lesson. It's up to you to discover which one it is and to learn the lesson the relationship was meant to teach you. Sometimes a person comes into your life to show you who you are. Relationships come to show you which direction you should travel and how to honor yourself or your partner. There are an infinite number of lessons that can be taught through a relationship.

Oftentimes, we have a perception of ourselves that isn't true, correct or precise. An intimate partner can reveal new data about who you are. You may have considered yourself the cool, fun person, but the relationship may reveal a nagging, overbearing person who pouts and manipulates to get what they want.

Intimate partners will push your buttons and show you things about your personality that you may not have known was there. Relationships will show you not only who you are, but also how you behave when you aren't in control. They can also reveal your ability to compromise or how you react to betrayal, disappointment, deception and the loss of a love.

Sometimes, it's a lover who will introduce you to a part of yourself that you didn't know existed. Other times a partner comes into your life to prepare you for the one, or teach you something that you will need to know to make the next relationship successful. For instance, your lover may teach you to relax and trust, not to snoop, hold on too tight, fight fair, to communicate, or not assume your partner knows what you want or need. Sometimes he/she will come into your life to build up your confidence and teach you your worth. There are many lessons that love and loss of love can teach.

43

Seasonal relationships usually transition you and make you keenly aware of what you want and don't want. These relationships help you to clarify your desires. For instance, you might think you want the captain of the football team, and you might start a relationship with him only to discover that the baggage that comes with him is too heavy. All the other girls that are lined up to take your place could make you feel disposable. The aggression in him may be too intense. His primary interest may be sports and you two don't have any other things that commonly unite you. You may discover that you want more out of the relationship than he can give. A relationship like this may teach you that the football type is great to look at but he may lack the substance and sensitivity that you're interested in. You may then further clarify your wants and desires, and realize that you need a beautiful, wonderful nerd that can have the deep conversations that you desire and is gentle and sensitive to our needs.

Even though the relationship does not stand the test of time it can still teach you about yourself, your needs and desires. Every relationship was not meant to be happily ever after. Sometimes it's merely a learning experience that provides valuable information and insights about what you need as opposed to what you want.

To learn the lessons that the relationship came to teach, you have to know when the relationship has run its course. When the relationship ends it can also act as an opportunity to learn how you handle break-ups. When a relationship ends, do you go to a crazy place, a depressed place, an introspection place, a desperate place or a pleading place? Who are you in the face of relationship disappointment? Do you prepare to boil rabbits or chase him/her down with your car? Do you take to your bed for days on end, eat ice cream in your pajamas and listen to sad music? Do you take the time to analyze what went wrong, learn from it and vow to be a better you as a result? Or do you immediately go on the prowl for a replacement?

Your assignment for today is to take some time and analyze your most recent relationships.

44

- What did each one teach you?
- What was the reason for each?
- Was the relationship transitional?
- What did the relationships have in common?
- Who were you in these relationships?
- How were the relationships different?
- How were you different?

The purpose of this exercise isn't to cast blame or bash anyone. The purpose is to see your relationship patterns and acknowledge them in an attempt to make you a better person, by recognizing the similarities in the emotion, characteristics, body types, attentiveness, work ethics and so forth.

You may see patterns that you never knew existed. You may recognize that you always seem to choose men/women who ignore you, are obsessed with their work or who cannot love you in a way that's important to you. You may learn that you were overbearing. Most importantly you may learn that you have some personal development that needs to be completed.

45

DAY 11
Knowing the Unknown
I SEE YOU

The fact that you are the one who will teach people how to treat you has been stated several times. It's the lesson I want you to learn above all others. However, partners aren't the only ones that can mistreat you. Ask yourself this: How have you mistreated you? What things do you do daily that don't promote the best you?

Do you

- Eat too much or improperly?
- Drink too much?
- Do drugs?
- Have unprotected sex, premature sex or sex for sport?
- Sacrifice your feelings, wants or needs for others?
- Have negative self-talk: "I'm too dumb to love," "I'm too fat" "No one can love me?"
- Give away yourself and your resources without expecting or wanting anything in return?
- Enter known relationship triangles?
- Refrain from speaking up for yourself?
- Say yes, when you know you should say NO?

All these things are forms of self-abuse, self-sacrificing or sabotaging behavior. You might not see it as abuse, but anything that you do to your mind or body that does not promote life, love or longevity is abusive. It's abusive to your lungs to fill them with smoke or toxic substances. It's abusive to your body to feed it improperly. You are your lover's first teacher, a person interested in you watches you, sees how you treat yourself and how you allow others to treat you. He/she gathers the information, takes copious notes and he/she can then gauge his/her treatments and responses to you accordingly.

It's extremely important for you to look very carefully at your actions and how those actions signal others to treat you. Make a list of the ways you mistreat yourself. What things do you do to yourself that are destructive? What are the things that you do to yourself that a person in love with themselves wouldn't do?

The bottom line is, if you want to be treated lovingly then you must treat yourself lovingly. You have to find the source of your mistreatment or self-abuse, acknowledge it and cure it. To cure these patterns you have to detect who established these patterns in you that keep you on a merry-go-round looking for love. How did you feel about yourself as a child, a teenager or young adult? What led you to believe this? And how have you abused yourself as a result?

Have you ever wondered how a guy/girl can walk into a gathering of people and know how to pick that person who will accept their abusive behavior or give everything and not expect anything in return? The predators know how to zone into the right person by seeing the behavioral clues and how they treat themselves. They don't choose the self-assured person who has self-esteem and demands to be treated well. They choose the person who is just glad to get some attention, any attention, even if it is abusive.

The good news is that, no matter the source of your self-abuse, it can be healed and left in the past! It's up to you now to decide to live better, do better, love better and be better. It's a hard lesson but it has to be learned if you don't want to keep repeating the same unfulfilling relationships. Start by asking yourself the questions above. Be completely honest, this is your time to shine and claim the life and the love that you deserve.

Get clear answers for the reasons this all started. Sit with it, allow yourself to feel the pain of it and make a new decision. A decision to love you and most importantly to treat yourself better. Don't try to make all the changes at one time, make small changes 30 days at a time. You can make a list of the things that you want to work on. Take one item on that list and decide to work on it for 30 days.

For example, one of the things on your list may be that you don't eat well or you eat too much. Maybe a solution would be that you'll eat a salad and vegetables every Wednesday. Or if smoking is on your list of how you mistreat yourself, decide that you aren't going to smoke until noon or decide that you're going to get an electronic cigarette.

You decide how you want to work on each issue. Sometimes small steps are easier to maintain. Work on one issue for 30 days, modifying it as you see fit. Notice the feelings and emotions that arise as a result of your efforts. Say loving things to yourself as you develop the self-love muscle.

This process is trial and error until you find the success you need. After 30 days, either vow to do more work on this one issue if it's something major, or add another item from your list. Next it might be exercise. Vow to walk 20 minutes every Sunday or twice a week. The most important thing is to treat yourself with loving kindness. Don't let the past keep you from being happy now or in the future.

Make gradual and small changes that you can keep up with and please don't use making these changes as another form of abuse by being too hard on yourself. These habits and patterns have been around for a long time and probably will take a little while to make progress. This isn't a precise science but you and your commitment are the only things that can make it work.

DAY 12
The Honesty Muscle
The GOOD, BAD and the UGLY

Choosing the wrong lover can also be a part of a person's self-abuse. It can be a self-fulfilling prophecy to subconsciously choose the wrong person in order to prove that you are unlovable. If a break-through is really what you want, you have to be willing to tell yourself the good, the bad and the ugly about you, your past and how that past influences you today. Telling your truth can be the most loving thing you ever do for yourself. It releases you from a self-imposed prison that can have you chasing your tail.

A woman I worked with years ago, came to me saying that she wanted to get married and have children. It was not an uncommon request for a woman over thirty. As we explored her history, she admitted that she had a series of relationships with men who were all either married or in committed relationships.

It's obvious to most people that if you want to be married you have to date a single man who is capable of marrying you. As we explored her history I discovered that her mother left her father when she was four. She left with a man that was also married and they started a life together in another state. Her father raised her alone until he eventually got remarried, when she was eleven. Her father was an excellent provider and gave her everything she needed and wanted but he was never around to enjoy life with her because he worked almost every day. At first she spent her time with her aging grandmother, who parked her in front of the television. Later her time was spent with her stepmother, whom she adored. She tried and tried to get her father's attention, but was virtually ignored. She craved love but always seemed to be an outsider in her own home.

Fast forward twenty years and she has found herself in a relationship with a married man. She believed that one day he would wake up and

49

realize that he couldn't live without her and leave his wife. Her partner gave her beautiful things and she was well provided for but she was lonely. Each day and year that passed she relived the pain she felt as a child growing up. She re-created in her intimate relationships that desire she had for her father's attention. There were glimpses of promise in the process, but ultimately she was left feeling unloved, ignored and left out. Sometimes, the issues seem to be common sense, but emotionally they were everything but.

Sometimes patterns that are clear to everyone else may be hidden from the individual. It took her years of waiting to finally realize that her lover was never going to leave his wife. I believe that he genuinely loved her, yet she was alone, always waiting for an opportunity for a few stolen moments.

In order to find true self-love and a loving life partner you will have to tell your the truth, which includes: good, bad and ugly! To make a new decision, she had to allow herself to see the truth and where her patterns came from. She had to admit her childhood had left her broken, lonely and love starved. Like her you have to be willing to admit where you're broken? If you don't acknowledge your brokenness you may never realize why you feel like you aren't enough. In keeping secrets and not acknowledging your life patterns you are allowing them to continue to control your life and keep you from the love you desire. It's self-sacrificial and it makes you prey to people with less than honorable intentions. Keeping secrets or not consciously acknowledging your past hurts will keep you in search of love from others who help you continue to abuse yourself.

In essence you are choosing heartbreak, because it may be all you know. I know that sounds ludicrous, but it's a choice. You choose heartbreak by:

- Choosing the wrong man/woman again and again,
- Overlooking obvious character flaws,
- Making excuses for the inexcusable,
- Seeing what you want to see rather than what is really there,

- Saying yes when your instincts and good sense say no,
- Accepting less than you know you deserve,
- Allowing someone into your life that comes to take rather than to share,
- Being too afraid to be alone and to say "No" when "No" is the ap propriate answer.

Sometimes in our quest to couple, we accept some things that we should sprint away from. Yet we invite them in, give them a key to our hearts and then act surprised when these relationships blow up in our faces. At some point you have to be willing to be alone rather than with the wrong person. Alone and working on loving you, nurturing you and preparing for the right person is a much better place than being with the wrong person, pretending that you don't know that the bottom is going to drop. If you are with the wrong person, there's no space in your life for the right person.

Your assignment for today is to make an honest assessment of your life, relationship choices and family patterns. It's time to tell your truth, the good, the bad, and the ugly.

D A Y 1 3
Leaving the Past
Making Love

Your previously made decisions can't be undone; the men/women that you have loved can't be erased. Each relationship has left its mark on your heart. However, anything or anyone that you chose in your past, you have the right to refuse now! It's your prerogative to change your mind. You can change your whole love pattern if you chose to do so. It's not particularly difficult. All it takes is a choice and a commitment to be different, love differently and create a better selection process.

I mentioned Heather Headley's song, "I wish" earlier. I love the lyrics to this song. She says,

"I wish I could go back to the day before we met and skip my regret."

Imagine if you had the chance to go back to the day before you met him/her and have a long conversation with yourself and say,

"Now tomorrow, you're going to meet a guy/girl who is handsome/beautiful, witty and sexy as hell. He/she looks like a different person, but believe me it's the same guy/girl. He/she is going to break your heart and treat you like sh*t. Don't be fooled by the smile and the laughter in his/her eyes, keep it moving. In fact, it's best to run when you see him/her."

Wouldn't that be a great power to have? I wish it was possible but it's not. The past cannot be unwritten. However, you can use those resulting lessons as learning experiences for where you are today. Over the next two days you are going to learn how to use the past to your advantage.

The first way to make great use of the past is to learn to strengthen your personal love muscle. The emphasis should be on the steps you can take to more adequately love you. Love attracts love, self doubt and depression attracts something totally different, toxic and dysfunctional. The questions that should be answered are:

- Can you forgive yourself for the past?
- Can you acknowledge your past relationships as learning tools to get you to a better place?
- Can you learn to do what is best for you even if it disappoints others?
- What does it take for you to feel special?
- What is lacking in your life and how can you give it to yourself?

By presenting your best self to the world you will attract better. The things you accept into your life depend on how you feel about yourself.

Your assignment for today is to take the time to do a short experiment. Go to a public place, a bar, nightclub, party, festival, or any place that people congregate. Try not to interact. Your assignment is to merely watch. Find the perfect spot and be the silent observer for an hour or two. Watch how people behave and ask yourself, who would most likely be attracted to that kind of behavior? What conclusions can you draw about a person who behaves in certain ways?

Spend a couple of hours just watching and then apply what you've learned to yourself and your own behavior.
- What do you think that people, who have observed your behavior over the years, have thought about you?
- What type of people do you think your behavior would attract?
- What vibe are you giving off?
- Are you that guy/girl who is trying too hard to get attention?
- Are you the party animal taking body shots?
- Are you the person cowering in the corner trying not to be seen?
- What would someone watching you most likely see and surmise about you?
- How has your behavior affected your relationship choices?
- Is the person your behavior will attract, the person you want or need?

Sometimes after you have had bad relationships for so long it's hard to believe that something different, better or more fulfilling can exist. Reassure yourself that it can. Spend some time trying to clarify what your needs are in a relationship. Determine if there are any contradictions between who you present yourself to be and who you really are. Develop a plan to make sure your behavior tells the truth about who you are.

Today, I hope you recognize the value in you, the love in you and what you have to offer another person that will be nourishing, supportive and loving. If you recognize your value, you can teach others to recognize your value as well. It starts by knowing you, especially the previously unknown parts. Instead of comparing yourself to a some idea of beauty that some magazine said was worthy of love, acknowledge your truth and learn to love what you see in the mirror. The goal today and everyday is to completely love yourself. Love YOU, in all your glory.

DAY 14
Using the Past for Inspiration
Kissing Frogs

The second step in learning to use your past to your advantage is using it to recognize Mr./Ms. Wrong. When you learn to accept yourself, who you really are, and acknowledge the good and bad things that have happened to create the person that you are, then you will be much more likely to see and acknowledge who others truly are. When you accept and put forward your authentic self and realize what type of person your behavior may attract, you will be less likely to be lulled into seeing facades and disingenuous people. When you are true to who you are, you will be able to see and accept others for who and what they are.

When trying to couple, it's not uncommon to overlook very important things because *we want what we want, regardless of the depravity that may accompany what we want.* Deep down in each relationship you probably knew exactly who you were attempting to love and that it would most likely end badly. I've asked clients, friends and family, who had failed relationships if there were any indications from the beginning that their relationship would not last. I was not shocked that the large majority of them said that they knew about and chose to overlook major or minor character flaws in their partner. Several men/women I talked to said, "I thought I could change them!", "I thought if I showed them how much I loved them, surely they would grow to love me too," or "I thought once we had children he/she would settle down."

It's common for people who love someone to try to make every effort to impress the object of their affection and try to do anything and everything to make that person love them too. A person will try manipulation, control, blackmail, con games, self-depriving acts, sexually explicit behavior, etc. Everything goes when they are trying to get a person to love them.

55

Trying to capture someone's heart can be an obsession for some people because, as we previously discussed, they're trying to work out old childhood drama through their present relationships. They work insanely, doing the same things over and over again trying to prove they are worthy of love.

The cycle can be broken by acknowledging who you really are, your brokenness, despair, heartaches, and learning from the past. In order to make a good relationship decisions you have to understand your own psyche, the reason, season and lesson from your past relationships, why certain relationships help you to work out your family patterns and why others help support your feelings of inadequacy. If you don't learn from your mistakes, it's very easy to repeat them over and over again. Sometimes you think you've learned and you may find yourself in yet another destructive relationship. If you become aware that the relationship is destructive, you have to decide whether to stay and suffer or to leave immediately.

I call this the one-way street scenario. Say you are driving down the street and you notice that all the other cars are going in the opposite direction. Then you look and there are indeed signs that indicate that you are on a one-way street, traveling the wrong direction. What do you do? Do you try to proceed cautiously, telling yourself that nothing is coming? Do you try to see if you can make it to the next block without a collision? Do you "hope" and "pray" for the best? Or do you put your flashers on and immediately find a place to turn around?

The answer is of course up to you. I'm always amazed at the people who will continue in a relationship that's headed down a one-way street in the wrong direction. They ignore the danger. When you make the decision to continue, your life is in your own hands and it is no longer the lover who did you wrong. You are doing yourself wrong. It's clearly your decisions to continue on an unsafe path that has proven detrimental in the past and will most likely continue to be detrimental. Once you make this decision, you lose the ability to play the victim. At some point we all have to decide to take our heads out of the sand, and deal with the reality of our decisions.

We have to learn the lessons of the past and use the past as inspiration for a brighter future.

An example of this situation is in the story of a young woman I met five years ago. She had been married for seven years, had two kids and was committed to her family. Her husband had been a good family man hard working and loving. He was good with the kids and loved his family. During the economic downturn he lost his job and fell into a deep depression.

After being unemployed for over a year and taking a huge blow to his ego, he found relief in drugs. Drug use had been prominent in his family and it seemed that he had avoided the demon that destroyed his family and sent two of his brothers to prison. After vowing to not follow in the footsteps of so many of his family members, he found himself drug addicted. His wife discovered that her husband was addicted to crystal meth. She loved him and said she couldn't leave him; she had vowed for better or worse. With the full knowledge that she was in a relationship with a drug addict who refused to go to treatment, she continued supporting and enabling him. She seemed shocked to discover that he had spent all the money in the checking account and pawned many of the family's valuables. She became angry with me when I told her, "that's what addicts do".

Months later she revealed that her father was an alcoholic and that she felt like she was living her mother's life rather than her own. Even though she consciously said she would never date a man like her father, subconsciously she had chosen him and she stayed just as her mother had. I'm not saying that she should have immediately left a seven-year relationship, but I'm saying that she should have acknowledged that her husband had a drug problem and protected her family and their resources. Her choice was to create a situation where she enabled his addiction, and she continued on a one-way street that led her family to financial ruin.

Patterns are easily repeated if you don't tell yourself the truth. It's imperative that you acknowledge to yourself the things that you don't want

57

to know. Denial is no longer an option. To counteract and overcome your family and relationship patterns you must acknowledge your bad judgment, oversights, past trauma, feelings of inadequacy and loving others more than you love yourself. It's time to forgive and live your best life.

Your assignment for today is to look back on your relationships and admit the times you continued on a one-way street going the wrong direction. Ask yourself when you realized you were going the wrong direction and how long it took you to turn around. Was it your choice to turn around or were you forced by your partner, a police officer or a collision to turn around?

DAY 15
Recognizing GOOD LOVE
20/20

Knowing the difference between "good love" and "bad love" is a skill that most people have to develop. The difference between "good love" and "bad love" is subjective; what I may consider bad love may feel normal to you. On the surface it would appear that it should be common sense to know "good love" from "bad love" and I'm sure that some would argue that all love is good. However, I have seen love be a destructive force in the lives of many.

It's sometimes hard to distinguish between good and bad love because so many of a person's decisions about love are made from the subconscious level. Another factor that makes it difficult is that so many potential partners wear carefully crafted facades and have masked intentions. I define "bad" love as the kind of love that's violent, controlling, demeaning, jealous, deceptive, full of rage, restrictive, painful, limiting, belittling, and/or abusive.

Good love depends on individual wants, needs, expectations, likes, dislikes, family patterns and sexual compatibility. Good love makes you feel valued, secure, supported, nourished, wanted and needed. Good love and bad love for each individual can be determined by your family patterns and personal expectations.

Oftentimes, there are things that are high on your list of requirements for good love that will bear no significant importance once you really explore what good love looks like for you. It will not matter if he/she is 5'8" or 6" or if he/she has brown eyes or blue, once all the important factors are examined. It would stand to reason that all of us would automatically know what "Good Love" looked and felt like. But most often, there have been a series of bad relationships that have colored your views. Our childhoods play a great role in what a good relationship looks like, but having addressed past influences and

59

learning to use the past as inspiration, we are now looking for ways to make sure that your love vision is 20/20.

For your assignment today, you will develop a process to help identify "good love" and "bad love" when you see it. Most of this process is internal. I'll give you a few steps to help you develop your plan, but the plan specifics and format is up to you. The first step in the "Recognizing Good Love Plan" is to interview couples you admire; couples who have been together for more than five years and divorced people you know or anyone that you trust and would like to get insights from. A word of caution: sometimes a relationship looks good on the outside to the general public but it can be a tragedy to the people in it. You have to look for subtle clues, knowing that sometimes you can learn just as much or possibly more from bad relationship examples as you can from good relationship examples. In your interviews, attempt to gain answers to these questions from the selected respondents:

- Did they know their relationship would last from the beginning? If so how did they know?
- How did they meet?
- Were they looking for love when they met?
- How do they nourish their relationship?
- What do they consider important in a good relationship?
- What are their relationship Deal Breakers?
- How do they keep their relationship alive and spontaneous?
- How do they settle and move on from disagreements, hurt feelings and disappointment?
- How do they nourish each other?
- How do they handle financial matters?
- How do they come to an agreement when they have differing opinions?
- How did they teach their partner to treat them?
- What were their short-term and long-term expectations?
- Were there difficult patches that they thought they would not get through?
- How did they make it?

60

- What are the components of a good relationship?
- What advice can they give you to know the difference between "good" love and "bad" love?

If any of the people whom you interview knows you well, ask them for their insights into your relationships. If they don't know you well then ask someone who does. Ask them about you personally and the relationship choices that they have observed.

- Do they believe you've made good relationship decisions?
- Have they seen patterns or similarities in the relationships you have chosen?
- Do they believe you treat yourself lovingly?
- How do they think you can improve?
- What behavior do they think you need to change?

If you want a relationship breakthrough you're going to have to learn what a good relationship looks like. It may be that you've never had a good relationship modeled for you. It means that you are going to have to be willing to hear the truth and don't discount it or make excuses for it. It might cause some momentary pain but it will not be nearly as painful as keeping the same habits and patterns for another ten, twenty or even thirty years.

DAY 16
A New Attitude
The Price is Wrong!!

A person can only learn so much from self introspection, at some point outside sources have to be sought to teach us about ourselves, who we have become as a result of life's ups and downs, heartbreaks and sorrows. Sometimes it's necessary to garner information from others so that we can see what's normal outside of the bubble that most of us live in. Normal for many is the way our parents did it and taught their children. Our lives are normal until we go out into the world and see how other people live, think and find ways to successfully couple. We cannot believe that there's only one normal and everyone has to adhere to it. Normality is in the eye of the beholder. Learning to understand other people's normal can be an eye opening and very gratifying experience. Learning different world views can broaden your horizons and enrich your life.

Holding on to a worldview that might not be shared by your partner may cost much more than the relationship can tolerate. If a healthy, happy relationship is what you want, there has to be some compromise. Both people have to be free to learn, grow and develop as individuals and as part of a couple and each partner may bring a different worldview to the table.

Sometimes in relationships, people throw all caution to the wind pursue and capture the person that they believe is just perfect; "the one". Then, because of their worldview, they try to mold their perfect person into what they think would be a MORE perfect person. The cost of who we have to be to keep this prized individual can be too high.

It's always problematic to try to force adults into a box that fits our liking. This may cause consequences that are heartbreaking. In most cases, seeking the prize is not about the prize or the person;

it's about trying to boost self-esteem or worthiness because some people believe that it's who is on their arm that gives them value rather than having their value be a reflection of their own worthiness and being. The uncompromising pursuit of the prized partner forces men and women to overlook flaws, clues and to disregard their good sense and intuition. When the prize is won on many occasions they realize it's really a victory that has cost them way too much.

A good example comes from my personal life; a person I was involved with had a totally different perspective and worldview than I did. It was clear that we cared about each other but our worldviews were very different. He grew up in a family where his mom never worked outside of the home. However, she worked tirelessly at home making sure every detail was perfect. The children didn't have chores, she did everything. She was overly obsessed with being the perfect mother and wife. She doted on her family; made sure a nutritious meal was always on the table when her family returned from school or work. She shined her husband's shoes and starched and ironed the families clothing. Her whole life was devoted to making sure that her family was well taken care of and they looked perfect in public. They were a very close knit family, every family function had its own formality. Their image was everything and it was a perfectly acceptable way to live.

Keep in mind that this was not wrong, just different from mine. The problem was that he wanted me to do the things his mother did and in the way she did them. To him, there was one way to fold towels or cook oatmeal and that way was how his mother did it. To comply meant that I would have to give up my dreams and aspirations to fit into the mold that he and his family had for what an acceptable wife.

I on the other hand, grew up with a mother who always worked. My father died unexpectedly from complications of diabetes when I was an infant. As a result, my mother was the breadwinner. She worked very hard to provide for her children and she taught us to dream big dreams, be independent and never give our personal power away. Our family focus was education and community service. We were raised to look out for neighbors and to share our limited resources with those in need.

63

Life was about giving back and making our community stronger.

He was old money and I was no money. While there was love and passion in this relationship, the cost of maintaining it was too high. He refused to budge on what he wanted and I was equally as stubborn. I was told in no uncertain terms what his expectations were if we were going to be successfully coupled. It was a devastatingly hard decision to make, but the part of me that loved who I was had to end the relationship. I was extremely independent and it was this character trait that attracted him but also the attribute that he fought to change.

Can you see any potential problems that might have developed in this coupling? Neither worldview was wrong, they were just different. How can two people with totally different childhood experiences, worldviews and agendas find a way to be a couple without losing who they are?

Your assignment for today is to explore what your worldview has taught you. Ask yourself, how has your worldview affected your relationships? How have you tried to modify your mates to fit your idea of right and wrong? Or has a partner tried to change you to make you comply to their worldview? Are you and your new mate willing to compromise your worldview and understand the different ways of being and doing that might arise in your new relationships? The answer should be yes of course, but this attitude of exploration takes work, commitment, and mutual respect. As you explore the dating pool, you will find a myriad of worldviews. Before you consider them wrong, take the time to understand and examine your own worldview for possible ways to compromise and embrace the traditions of a new partner.

DAY 17
The Million Dollar Question

Most of us are born with a certain level of intuition. The strength of your intuition varies from person to person, but all of us have it. It can be our internal guiding system, but it has to be acknowledged and developed. Today, we are going to learn how to ask the million dollar questions and hopefully begin to use our intuition more.

Looking back, what could you have asked yourself that would have saved you from your last relationship and the heartbreak that followed?

• What can you ask yourself to make sure that you don't select a new partner using the same criteria that you've used in the past?

• What questions can you ask yourself to make sure that familial patterns aren't making the selections instead of your rational conscious mind?

What do you need to know immediately? Think about what information would be most useful for you to know before you get involved with a new partner. After you are clear about the nature and scope of your fact-finding mission, make a list of the questions that you need to ask at the beginning of a relationship that will clue you to delegate him/her to the friend zone, to relax and let the relationship develop organically, walk away or to run.

Prepare your checklist before your hormones are raging and you are mesmerized by those dimples and the smile that could stop traffic. Identify the things that are important to you, those questions that will unearth the information that matters to you. Remember that most people tell you everything you need to know within the first few hours of conversation, you just need to know what questions to ask and how to listen.

65

Oftentimes the important questions aren't asked until the relationship has become both physical and emotional. By that time it's truly too late. Before a new relationship is on your radar make sure your list of questions is formulated and committed to memory, just in case you can't stop looking into those eyes, or wondering how those tight abs feel. Before you get lost in his/her cologne, open the "need to know" file in your brain and ask the questions you have committed to memory for a situation like this. Know that most jerks don't look like jerks from the beginning. Mr./Ms. wrong is usually quite captivating.

Your goal is to know your patterns, what you want and need, what a good relationship feels like to you and the questions to ask yourself to see if the person in front of you is going to take you closer to your goals or further away. Below are a few questions to get you started. Ask these questions after you have had a couple of dates and your interest in this person is growing.

- Is anything about this person familiar to me?
- What feelings come up for me?
- What do I really believe the outcome of this relationship will be?
- Will this relationship most likely end up being another way for me to abuse myself?
- Is this the person that I would choose for the new me, or does this feel like a partner for the old me?
- How will this person fit into my plans, goals?
- Can I be my authentic self with him/her?
- Is this the same man/woman with a different name?
- Why am I attracted to him/her?
- What would most likely be the reason, season and lesson for this relationship?

You can have as many or as few questions as you want. The goal is to go into any future relationship fully aware of what your needs are, what goals you plan to achieve, what your past relationship patterns have been and how to make new and more productive, supportive and nourishing decisions.

Please don't meet someone and immediately pull out a list of questions and interview him/her like Barbara Walters. Gradually work your questions into the normal flow of the conversation or just listen. Your questions may be answered within normal conversation. Actively listening and asking clarification questions will provide many of answers that you seek.

A word of caution: you will never find a perfect person, everyone you meet will have flaws and rough places where growth may be necessary, so make sure you weigh the good and the bad and make a wise decision. People with rough edges are much different than abusive people with ulterior motives. Make sure you look realistically because requiring perfection means you need to be perfect. What you are trying to avoid are major character flaws and incompatibility issues, people who make you feel as if you are not enough, people who come to take from you rather than to share with you.

Before you get involved in a new relationship here are some basic questions that might provide valuable information from a prospective partner.

- Do you like children?
- What do you think the man's and woman's role is in a relationship?
- What type of men/women are you normally attracted to?
- What if you really wanted something and your partner disagreed, how would you resolve the dispute?
- Where have you gone wrong in previous relationships?
- What does a good relationship look like to you?
- How do you make your partner feel special?
- When you are angry or disappointed how do you express it?
- Is there ever an appropriate time for hitting or name-calling, abuse or sexual assault?
- How should disagreements be handled?
- What was your childhood like?

Your assignment for today is to add your question to this list. Make every attempt to get the questions answered that are important to you. Check for compatibility by answering the same questions for yourself.

67

Listen carefully and learn not to sweat the small stuff. So what if he/she wears colorful socks? If he/she is loving, supportive and giving, and you feel good and valued when you are with him/her, then colorful socks aren't that important.

Just like all transformations, this transformation starts in your mind and is reinforced by your positive and repetitive behavior. The exercise where you were instructed to watch people's behavior and the reaction others had to them will be helpful in this process as we take a closer look at your behavior and how you present yourself to the world.

First, what behaviors limit you and give others an image of you that's not accurate?
- Are you the girl/guy that dresses provocatively and attracts the kind of attention that you don't want?
- Are you the shy person that's easily overlooked?
- Who are you?
- And how do you become a better more authentic version of your self?

Be mindful of your behavior as you present yourself to the eligible population of single men/women. Make sure you present yourself in a fashion that's honest, authentic and desirable. If you want to have a different type of person to couple with then you have to be a different kind of you, the real you. You have to present yourself in the way that will set the parameters for how you want to be treated, two weeks from now or five years from now. If you want to be treated like a lady/gentleman, act like a lady/gentleman, not the drunk at the bar that never knows when enough is enough.

If you aren't sure of what a lady/gentleman should act like then find some ladies or gentlemen that represent the type of womanhood/manhood that you admire. Watch them, ask them for advice and make the adjustments in your life to support the truth of who you are. But always be authentic, don't pretend to be church lady or deacon when you know you like to drink beer from the bottle, curse like a sailor, and break all the commandments on any given day. If it means going back to school to be who you want to be, losing weight, or dressing differently, do it. Make the changes that make you feel your best so that you will find a partner that wants to be the best for you.

Sometimes transitions are tricky. You don't want to try too hard, you just want to get to the point where you are true to yourself and your outside reflects who you truly are and what you want to present to the world. The only way you can find someone that's truly compatible with you is to be completely and unapologetically yourself. You want to attract a lover who adores who you are and not an image that you have portrayed that is not an accurate depiction of who you truly are.

I wish I had a dime for every time a man or woman told me he/she was like this when we met, but has since changed and now I no longer recognize this person. An individual can only keep up a facade for so long before the armor starts to crack and the multiple personalities and personas begin to seep out. That's why it's so important when you meet a potential partner to gather all the available information and take careful inventory of the cracks in their armor and personal behavioral inconsistencies as well as your own.

Always be true to who you are and see clearly who is in front of you. Look at all the information presented, examine it, analyze it, and make sure that you're willing to put up with this trait, habit, or idiosyncrasy five or ten years from now should this become a long-term relationship. And know that the person sitting across from you is examining your armor and looking for cracks and behavior inconsistencies in you. This person is carefully reviewing your resume and checking your references. You want to have the best possible partner for you, but you also have to be the best possible partner. The quest for authenticity means that you have to catch any discrepancies in you, address them and correct them.

It's not unusual to think we present ourselves one way, but others perceive your actions and demeanor as something totally different. How do you begin to portray an image that's accurate?

The first step is to be completely honest, say what you mean and mean what you say. You can speak your truth without being intentionally hurtful, disrespectful or rude.

As I stated before my mother has given me thousands of pieces of good advice, but one piece of advice always stands out. She said "Always start out the way you plan to finish." This is clearly one of the best things she ever taught me. So I will pass it on to you, again. If you plan to do all the cooking, cleaning, and laundry, then start that way. If you plan to always pay for your partner's expensive taste, start that way. If your partner goes missing for days and you are waiting with open arms whenever he/she decides to return, then start that way. If you plan to always be perfectly agreeable and not speak your mind or complain, then start that way. But remember you are teaching your partner that this behavior is acceptable to you.

If you are completely honest with yourself, you can admit that some of the heartbreak you have experienced was directly associated with your calculated choices? You knew what you were getting was not what you needed.

Once you've worked on yourself to become the best you, then ask yourself what type of man/woman do you need to help you continue to be the best you. Remember if you continue to hide your true self and accept what you always had, you are headed for another heartbreaking scenario. Never forget that there's someone who will love you just the way you are with all your faults, defects and imperfections.

Your assignment for today is to take an inner inventory of who you really are and who you want to become. What steps do you have to take to close the gap between where you are and where you want to be? Develop an action plan.

71

DAY 19
Sphere of Influence
Blind Spots

When it comes to making good relationship choices sometimes there can be blind spots in your thinking and behavior. Blind spots can be dangerous and you have to do whatever you can to minimize them. You must keep in mind however that some blind spots will always exist.

This became crystal clear to me while taking a road trip with my sister in her new Lincoln MKS. I fell in love with one of the new car's features, the lane change assistance feature. If there's a car or object too close to you that might cause a collision, the lane change assistant notifies you with a beep or a verbal notification to let you know that there is danger if you continue on that path. This lane change assistance was designed to cover your blind spots. I really liked it and it made me think how great it would be if we had that kind of assistance in our daily lives.

Sometimes wisdom and insights come from a variety of unlikely sources, even automobile technology. The Lane Change Assistant caused me to wonder, what it would be like if there was a mechanism that would warn you of impending relationship danger. I think most single people would line up to get one. Can you imagine going into a holiday party and spotting a gorgeous guy or girl and having the lane change assistant go off? At first barely audible and then louder and louder as you approach Mr./Ms. wrong. That could be a hilarious comedy skit for Saturday Night Live, but it could also be very useful in real life. However there is no relationship lane change assistant or iPhone app (to my knowledge) that warns you of approaching relationship danger. Even though this does not exist on the open market, you can create your own system that will warn you about obvious relationship danger.

72

The first element in developing this system is being keenly aware of your past family issues, relationship blunders and how you want to choose differently. This will give you some tools to spot the most obvious nuisances that invade your relationship pool. The next element is the list of questions that you developed to root out characteristics and flaws that might not be as easily spotted.

The third element is your Sphere of Influence, which consists of the people who love you, support you, and wish the very best for you. Your Sphere of Influence can include the supportive aunt, that girlfriend that always comes when you call and holds the box of tissue while you cry uncontrollably, or the co-worker that tries to fix you up with the nice guys and warns you about the bad ones. You have to know without a shadow of a doubt who has your best interest at heart and who wants to see you soar, as opposed to those who want to control you. You have to know the people who support you and cry you through one heartache after another. They're the people who have watched and tried to warn you that you were on the wrong path. In hindsight you realize that they have been right time after time, even though you are reluctant to admit it. These people should be included in your Sphere of Influence list. Think about all the warnings that you've ignored and all the heartache, pain and frustration that you've had to endure as a result of not listening to these people.

Your Sphere of Influence can be a very valuable tool if you learn to use it correctly. Solicit their help; ask them what patterns they see as problems in your life and if they will agree to point them out to you when they see you going in a direction that is counterproductive to your expressed goals. The key is that you have to learn to listen and value their input. I'm not saying that you should cease thinking for yourself, but you should be able to recognize and consider good advice from the people who have proven that they genuinely love you and have your back.

Bear in mind that a passenger in the car can sometimes see a blind spot better than the driver. Create an agreement with your Sphere of Influence to support you in the process of your relationship makeover. Require that they will tell you openly and honestly if they see a train wreck

73

coming. Then you should agree to take the information, examine it and carefully see what is there rather than what you want to see. Please resist the temptation to discard their observations or to prove them wrong. Agree to hear their insights and not shoot the messenger. You don't have to agree with their advice but you must listen to it. This process does not mean that you let someone else pick a partner for you. On the other hand, it does mean that you will listen to the people you chose if they see one of your choices going wrong and they can tell you freely without fear of your response.

Think back to the times when your mom, dad or friend warned you about someone you were involved with but you chose not to listen, yet they were proven right. You didn't think they knew what they were talking about but they did. You had a blind spot, but your Sphere of Influence saw it very clearly. Find out what they saw and learn how to see it for yourself. Some of it is a natural progression that comes with age, however there are tips and clues that you can learn that will begin to minimize your blind spots.

Set up game rules where your Sphere of Influence can speak honestly without the threat of you getting angry, causing a scene or generally behaving badly. Agree to entertain the information that they provide, listen and acknowledge that if you were good at seeing the writing on the wall you wouldn't be reading this book.

On the other hand, your Sphere of Influence does not get to dictate your life or decide who you can and cannot date. Think of them as your consultants. They will present their observations and you will take their comments under advisement. They will clearly articulate their concerns in a supportive and loving fashion and you have to be able to see clearly that the information they provide is given to increase your awareness and your best good and personal growth., The final decision, however, is always yours.

Your assignment for today is to decide who will serve as your Sphere of Influence consultants.

74

DAY 20
Evaluating your needs
Spinach or Ice Cream

Wants and Needs are two totally different things. It would be a wonderful occurrence if we always wanted the things we needed. Oftentimes, we tell ourselves that what we want is what we need. Sometimes our wants and needs are confused and we struggle to differentiate between the two. It takes an immense amount of awareness to learn to want what we need.

For instance, I know that to eat a healthy diet I need vegetables, fruits, nuts, and whole grains. These are the things I NEED as part of a healthy diet. However, what I most often want is cake, ice cream, salty snacks and fried foods. Every day I have to make a decision between the things I want and the things I need. It would be great, if I craved spinach rather than ice cream, but the fact of the matter is that I have to make a very conscious decision to choose my needs over my wants. That's not to say that sometimes my wants don't overrule my needs. I can have ice cream, but in moderation.

The same phenomenon exists in the relationship world. There's a certain type of guy/girl that we like who will stimulate all of our senses and desires. However, the person that we want might be just as dangerous to our system, sensibilities and weight, as eating a quart of ice cream every day.

When looking for possible options for coupling, be able to identify wants (ice cream) or needs (spinach). You want a man/woman that's exciting and fun. Think of it as your favorite flavor of ice cream (or whatever is decadent that you love, if you don't like ice cream). There's something about the ice cream that excites you and makes you feel alive. However, the feeling that you get with the ice cream is short lived. It can add extra weight and the sugar can cause disease and a multitude of health issues.

75

In comparison, the spinach is kind of bland. It's healthy for you but not as tasty, yet it's long-term effects on the body are undeniable. The spinach can be nourishing, it can support the immune system, help lower the incidence of certain diseases and it's good for your overall health. But when faced with the decision of what to choose, it can be a difficult choice between ice cream or spinach. Either one you choose can have long term effects. The goal is to turn the spinach you need into what you want. In other words, you have to retrain your mind to want what's good for you. It doesn't mean that you can never have ice cream, but for health reasons it's best to eat it in moderation, along with a healthy balanced diet. And if you do chose the ice cream you have to admit to yourself, that you may be making an unwise decision, which has definite consequences.

One way to close the gap between wants and needs is to view short-term effects with long-term effects. Sure the ice cream is going to be good for a very short time, but the long-term effects can be disastrous. It's been said, "A minute on the lips is a lifetime on the hips." The question then becomes, "Do I want this short-term pleasure that may result in many painful consequences or do I want what will support and nourish my long term health and longevity?"

There's a nutritional battle that takes place every day. You want someone that's going to be there for you through the good and the bad, but you want to follow the excitement of Mr./Ms. wrong. You need a man/woman to treat you well but you want the bad boy/girl to excite you and take you on a roller coaster ride of emotions. You need loyalty and respect, but you want fun and adventure that may bring with it a level of danger. You want a dedicated spouse and mother/father for your children, but you also want the irresponsibility and intrigue of Mr./Ms. wrong. It's a tough decision sometimes, but your very life, hopes and dreams depends on whether you make the correct choice.

I'm amazed at how often people spend their time gambling and hoping and praying that what they want is what they need. Every decision we make in life comes with consequences. An interesting observation is that most of the time the things we are looking for in others is what we need to cultivate within ourselves. If you want excitement, be the excitement you crave. Make things happen for yourself and enjoy your life in the process.

Delayed gratification can be useful and adults are forced to learn this. Children who have not developed a strong sense of responsibility and the ability to look at long-term effects are swayed by the urgency of what they want now. They don't have the mental capacity or life experience to reason things through and examine the possible incidents and consequences that may result from eating a quart of ice cream every day. They just want what they want, something shiny and new. But as we grow up and see the consequences of our actions we usually put it all into perspective and realize that if I chose this, in the long run I'm most likely going to get this. As we age, we can no longer plead ignorance of the possible situations that making wrong relationship choices can bring. The choice is yours. Will it be ice cream or spinach?

Your assignment for today is to describe what spinach (your needs) looks like in a relationship for you and what ice cream (your wants) looks like for you. Decide which is more important to you and how you can get what you want and what you need.

DAY 21
The Makeover
Until Today

Today is the makeover day, not the do over day. This makeover will not include shopping for a new wardrobe, or changing your hairstyle or color. This is a heart makeover, where you get a chance to reprogram your heart. It's time to expel the toxic waste from all your bad relationships. This pollution has occupied space in your heart and mind for too long. It is time to prepare yourself for a love that's soothing for your soul and nurturing to your spirit. Whatever mistakes or miscalculations in judgment that have surrounded your romantic life are now over. The clock is now reset. Your romantic intentions for coupling starts anew with new goals and objections and new expectations. Today, you can change your mind. You will develop a new criteria that's based on your heart's desires. You've taken a personal relationship inventory. You've learned more about:

- Your dating patterns
- Your family patterns
- Your self-abusive ways
- What you want
- What you need
- Your worldview
- How you see yourself
- How others see you
- Who to go to when in doubt
- What questions to ask
- What to listen for

Armed with this knowledge, you know better and when you know better you do better. You have made a conscious decision to make over your love life, partner profile, agenda, wants, needs and blind spots. The partner that may have been acceptable to you six months ago, may not be acceptable to you today because you are clear about what you want and you know you deserve better than the options that have presented themselves in the past.

I had a good friend tell me, when discussing the problems in her relationship, "Well, Tom is bad but he isn't nearly as bad as Sam". This struck me. I'd known her for a long time and she was correct because the issues that she had with Tom were not as severe as the ones she had with Sam. That much was true. But what struck me was, she shouldn't be comparing bad to worse. The comparison should have been between bad and much better.

If you think you deserve much better than what you have received in the past, today is the time you need to express it, shout it, demand it and accept nothing less. Your mind should be made up based upon what you are willing to give, who you are willing to be and what you should expect to have in a partner. Now is the day to makeover your dream partner, the person you are willing to support, nourish, love and work side by side with to carve out the kind of life that the two of you desire and deserve.

There are just a few keys to help your makeover successful. The most important one is AWARENESS, Awareness and more awareness. You are now aware of why you chose who you chose, why you allowed what you allowed, and how you will makeover your dating narrative. Remember the past, because sometimes you have to look backward to move forward. The mistakes you have made serve as the foundation for your education and transformation.

Take some time and meditate on what kind of relationship you want. Do you want to have fun, travel, just keep things light or do you want a committed long-term relationship that leads to marriage. The decision is yours and you get to make the rules.

- What does your dream relationship look like?
- How does it make you feel?
- What kind of person is he/she?
- Who are you in this relationship?

- How do you love, support and nourish your partner?
- How are you loved supported and nourished by your partner?
- What do you have to learn to make a relationship like this successful?
- What are your Deal Breakers?
- What are your expectations?
- Where do you want this relationship to go?

Makeover your expectations and intentions; it's totally up to you. There will be times when you will have to listen to your Sphere of Influence and walk away. There will be times when you realize that what you have isn't what you were looking for. There will be times when you find exactly what you want and realize that it's not what you need. The key here is to be aware of what you want, what you need and what is comprisable and what is not. To position yourself for success you must be truthful, no more pretending. Time brings about a change and the change you desire has started in you.

Your assignment for today is to DREAM! Dream about the relationship you want and who you must be in that relationship. Makeover your expectations and goals and set your intentions for your relationship. SWEET DREAMS!

DAY 22
Have we Met
Profiling

Having learned all about yourself and your past relationships and deciding to makeover your romantic expectations, it's time to profile your Mr./Ms. Right. Yesterday you made over your relationship expectations, now it's time to profile your ideal mate. This is the occasion where profiling is needed, accepted and encouraged. The first step is to decide what issues are important to you: morality, sensitivity, honesty, sexuality, appearance the ways you want to be loved. In order to know your partner when you meet him/her, let's develop some identifying elements, criteria and ground rules that will help you recognize him/her.

Start with the questions below to begin profiling what you want, but a word of caution: This is a "Dream Mate" and your actual mate might not have everything on your list. By creating your list you'll discover that some of the things on your list may be unrealistic in the first place. The list is a starting point that will change, evolve and advance you toward the love of your life.

As you take time to ponder your profile, you'll tweak it and realize that some things are really not that important. Other things are comprisable, some things are Deal Breakers, other things are just plain laughable. The most important thing to consider is the person's character. Here are some questions for you to consider while developing your profile:

- Does he/she twist the rules to fit his/her morality?
- Does he/she believe that rules and laws don't apply to them?
- Does he/she think that it's okay to lie, cheat, and steal to get what they want?
- Is he/she honest always, or just when people are watching?
- Will he/she love you?

- Is this the kind of man/woman that you want your children to emulate?
- Is he/she considerate of anyone's need, other than his/her own?
- Are you likely to be ignored in this relationship?
- Are you likely to give more than you receive in this relationship?
- Will you be equal partners in this relationship?
- What type of person is he/she?
- What would he/she most likely do in his/her spare time?
- How would he/she react to a friend in need?
- Does he/she like children?
- Has he/she been married or divorced?
- What would he/she wear?
- What would he/she look like?
- Where would he/she most like go for fun?
- How would he/she treat you?
- What would his/her expectations of you be?
- How does he/she behave when he/she is angry?
- What does he/she believe about family?
- Is he/she faithful?
- Can you trust him/her?
- What are his/her motivations?
- What are his/her Deal Breakers?
- Does he/she like to laugh?
- Does he/she believe in social justice, women's rights, and equality?
- Is he/she religious or spiritual?
- What would his/her friends, family, and co-workers say about him/her?

Today you are free to create the profile that you want, whatever makes you happy. Nothing is written in stone, but you want to know what type of person you are looking for, you can watch and observe his actions and determine if he meets your particular profile. Keep your profile flexible change and adjust it where needed. Determine if your profile corresponds to the dream relationship that you composed yesterday.

DAY 23
Getting Realistic

Now since you spent yesterday designing the perfect mate, it's time to get realistic. The reality of relationships is that everyone has flaws; no one is perfect, and even with the best tools in the world you can still chose a jerk. Choosing correctly can be difficult because some people put their false face forward and it might be months before you discover that the great guy/girl who loves to listen to your grand-mother's stories has a mate and three kids in another state. Or it might be a month before you realize that he/she has lied to you every time he/she opens their mouth. In the real world people hide their true selves and their identity. Chris Rock said in a comedy routine that, "from the beginning you don't meet the person, you meet their representative." It's up to you to recognize the representative and make every attempt to meet the real person. I believe most people are honest and the ones who aren't are just lost souls in need of a breakthrough.

Even though the dishonest people are in the minority, you still have to look out for them because they can be found everywhere and they look just like the rest of us. They will be easier to distinguish with the tips you've picked up in the last twenty-two days. As a result you will be able to spot them easier and disengage early. As you are becoming clearer about what you want and need, this is the perfect time to start thinking about your "Deal Breakers." Those things that will not be tol-erated under any circumstances. Every individual should have some minimum standards that must be met before a person can enter their life.

When it comes to relationships, it should not be "anything goes." There should be some things that you now recognize that set off the alarm bells in your head. Some actions and behaviors from a potential partner should start to be clearly seen as obvious "Deal Breakers"

83

which are as easily viewed as fireworks. With the tools you've gathered, there should be specific words, actions, or patterns which will alert you that something is just not right. When you recognize certain patterns they should alert you to sprint away from this individual.

You have to be cautious about the people you meet. You want to give everyone the benefit of the doubt, but you also want to be cautious of who you invite into your life and your space. It's imperative that you LISTEN carefully and make mental notes of any inconsistencies in their story or persona. Be aware of your instincts and intuition. Don't ignore them when you get a warning, even if it's a slight discomfort. Take the time and listen to it, think of it as your internal lane change assistant. As you pay more and more attention to these subtle internal warnings, they will get stronger and stronger and guide you through relationship danger.

Think of yourself as a relationship detective, with the mission of finding the true love of your life. It's possible and quite probable that you will have to wade through the manure to find the right one. That's to be expected, but you must decide not to linger there too long. Be mindful of all the tools in your arsenal that are there to equip you to fight a battle that I know you can win. Don't be so anxious to believe a person that you forget to logically think things through. Listen, because hearing or not hearing can possibly take time out of your life and make you miss Mr./Ms. Right. Listen as if your life depended on it because in some cases, life has depended on the trustworthiness of a lover or spouse.

Think about all the men and women who have lost their lives in some sinister plot or murderous rage, concocted by their trusted spouse or significant other. Also be mindful of all those who have died from a disease they contracted from an unfaithful spouse. Furthermore, consider the number of financial disasters and bankruptcies that have resulted from spouses with secret lives or addictions. And if you don't consider anything else, think about the predators that you may bring into your home. We always tell our children about stranger danger, but what happens when you bring the dangerous predator into your home and serve your children to them on a platter. The most important thing you need to learn is when to RUN.

84

I'm always amazed by the number of times I've sat in front of the television watching the news to see another domestic violence situation play out with S.W.A.T. for the world to see. Most of the time, it's a husband or boyfriend murdering or maiming a wife and it comes out that she has endured various types of abuse for many, many years yet she stayed and accepted it. She trained him to think that it's okay to abuse her and after years and years of abuse, she wants to change a pattern that has been heavily embroidered into their relationship fabric. I always think, what would have happened if the first time he raised his voice or pushed her, she RAN at top speed to the nearest relationship exit and never looked back. I wonder how many "I'm sorry," and "I'll never do it again," she endured before she decided she couldn't take it anymore.

Learning when to run is a skill that can save your life one day. It's NEVER acceptable to be abused. Over the years, I've had too many women tell me, "He didn't mean to hurt me," "He was so sorry," "It only happens when he drinks," or "He is having problems at work." None of these excuses are adequate for receiving one harsh word, one slap or one punch. Not to mention years of it. At the first glimpse of any maltreatment, know when to RUN!!!!!!

Abuse isn't the only deal breaker in a relationship. Get realistic about all your Deal Breakers, what will you absolutely not tolerate under any circumstances? Drugs? Cheating? Maltreatment of your children? Stealing? Your Deal Breakers are these items that you absolutely refuse to compromise on, the things that automatically end the relationship. Both partners need to understand what the Deal Breakers are from the beginning so he/she cannot plead innocence. Deal breakers are the only items set in stone.

I hope physical characteristics are not among your Deal Breakers, because what a person looks like is minor and superficial. I understand some level of attraction is necessary, but it shouldn't be so stringent that you overlook a beautiful, loving individual that wants to love and treasure you, just because he/she won't make the cover of a magazine. Does it really matter how tall he/she is? It matters more to know that he/she will be in your corner.

85

It matters to know that he/she would be a good father/mother to your children and his/her example won't be a bad one for your children to learn from. Height, hair color or other superficial characteristics aren't important, what is important is that he/she will grow with you and support you and be your soft place to fall at the end of an excruciating day. It doesn't matter if his/her eyes are blue or brown. It matters that he/she sees you, loves you and makes your happiness his/her priority. It matter's that he/she loves you and makes sure you know it because of the big and little things that he/she does on a daily basis. It does not matter if there are calluses' in his/her hands, what matters is whether those hands hold your heart as treasure or as a recyclable.

The only things that matter are how you are loved, how you are treated, how you are accepted and respected. There was a beer commercial featuring Billy Dee Williams years ago, the catch phrase was, "Don't let the smooth taste fool you!" Of course, they were talking about the beer, but as I stated before, I get insights and inspiration from some very unlikely places. What the smooth taste means in this context is the "glitz and glamour" that fools you in relationships. Don't be fooled by someone telling you what you want to hear. Don't be fooled into thinking that a less attractive person has less value. Don't be fooled into thinking that money can buy you love or that a house is more important than a home. It would be great if we were all super models, but the fact of the matter is that we aren't. Don't be swayed by the money in his/her bank account. The money can't give you the support and encouragement you need; only the man/woman can. Please don't become mesmerized by expensive gifts and cars, these material things cannot provide comfort or hold your hand when you need a shoulder to cry on. Be swayed only by the value he/she puts on you as a person and as partner.

I've seen some very beautiful people who had ugly attitudes and gross personalities. They were disrespectful and presented themselves as entitled. I've also seen beautiful people who were such good people that it made them impossible not to be attracted to. Additionally, I've seen those who would be considered less attractive, who had a way of being that drew you in like a moth to a flame. Their persona was so strong that it was almost palpable.

86

I've also seen unattractive people who were bitter, resentful and mean spirited. The lesson is that all people are different and you have to look further than face value. You must consider the outer person and the inner person before you decide who is a keeper and who isn't.

Please don't judge people by their shell, it simply doesn't matter. Ask yourself, if you were incapacitated for some reason and your partner or spouse had to make life and death decisions about your life, what kind of person would you want to make those decisions for you? Would it matter if they were a 10, 7 or 5 on a rating scale if your life were in jeopardy? Sometimes, the love of your life will come in an unexpected package. Don't miss the blessing.

Your assignment for today is to revise your profile and your dream relationship. Start to think about your "Deal Breakers." It's time to get realistic and open your heart and your mind.

DAY 24
Knowing Your Worth

The key to taking a stand for you and what you want is knowing that you deserve to be happy and treated lovingly. You have to know that you deserve the undivided attention, commitment and love from a partner who knows your value as well as you do. It's easy to love others, but so many times we are self-sacrificing because we don't know that we deserve to be happy and that our needs and wants are just as important as those of our partners and family.

You should be in love with yourself and your partner. It's not cocky or conceited to love yourself, it's absolutely necessary. Love isn't something that's available for a few. "Good love" is available for us all. I believe that there is someone for everyone. You have to know they exist, search for them and when you find that person, nourish the relationship, support and grow with your partner.

Regardless of the situations that you've endured previously, you deserve "good love" now. I can say it a million times but you have to know it in your heart and soul. You have to open yourself up for it. I don't mean hanging out at the bar every night, looking for love in a bottle or in meaningless sex. I mean you have to open your mind and your heart to what the universe wants to send you. But if you don't know you deserve this great gift, you will not be able to receive it. You will question it, sabotage it and grieve it once it's gone. It's a true blessing to find someone who loves you, bad hair days, and all.

To open your heart and mind for love, you have to first practice loving you, treating yourself well and making you a priority in your life. I've talked to so many women/men who have time for everything and everyone accept themselves. Your lover's first clues of how to treat you are going to come from you, so without a shadow of a doubt you have to do loving things for yourself. You have to take time to nourish your spirit, heal your wounds and strive for the love you deserve.

Sometimes, loving yourself may mean that there are relationships and people that you have to let go of. If you have people who drain your energy, take from you and never repay, it may be time to renegotiate the relationship or separate from it entirely. If they make you feel less than a special and unique gift from God, you might have to let them go. You are looking for people and relationships that help to nurture and support you. If you find yourself always the one giving and not receiving then for the sake of your own success, it may be time for you to cut your ties. You deserve to get back what you give. You deserve to be happy. You deserve to be supported and nourished. You deserve to have energy restored instead of always drained. You deserve the arms of someone who loves you.

Another one of my unusual insights came from a routine by comedian Chris Rock. I can't remember the exact quote but he said something to the effect that 90% of the women want 10% of the men and vice versa. His explanation was comical, but when you break it down and examine it, there's a lot of truth to that statement. Most people are looking for someone beautiful, successful and with money. Doctors, lawyers, athletes, and/or some other high profile career. The 10% people can be shallow because they have so many opportunities at relationships that they don't feel they have to be faithful or respectful. They know partners, for them can be plentiful and disposable. They know when one guy or girl leaves, 100 other women/men are lined up to take their place. In the minds of some of the 10% types, partners who flock to them are not valuable assets, they're merely the flavor of the week. While everyone is chasing the 10%, millions of great girls and guys, who may not have the bling or the model looks are passed over and discounted because they don't fit the profile of the rich and famous.

Take time to look at the number of women who line up to get backstage to see a performer or band. Consider all the women who are waiting for the bus or in the hotel lobby when some professional team comes to a city to play a game. Or all the people waiting and hoping to get into the VIP in the nightclub. Think of all the single women flirting and stalking the single doctor, lawyer, business-person, or captain of industry, while ignoring the accountant, cable installer, or member of the 90% class.

The numbers are staggering. The 10% (the beautiful and successful people) are aware that these groupies have put themselves into a position, where they can be easily used and they have no problem using them and disposing of them, never to be thought of again. Rarely does this scenario turn into a long term loving relationship, based on mutual admiration and respect. And the spouses who are lucky enough to marry one of the 10% types are sometimes forced to endure maltreatment and numerous affairs.

What do you think would happen if the 90% put their energy into being the best they can be and attracting a great life partner in the 90% of the opposite sex? When looking for love, try to remember to keep your eyes open for the 90% that might have previously gone unnoticed. You don't deserve to be one of many, you are not a recyclable, you are a treasure that some special person cannot even imagine living without.

Love yourself enough to make some adjustments in your life for things that are good and right and sweet and kind. Be cautions however when you are looking for people to support you. Make sure that you don't become the one that takes rather than gives. Be the kind of person you want to meet. When you consider someone for coupling make sure you see the heart rather than the physical attributes and financial status. Looks will surely change over time and fortunes are often made and lost. It's the heart that will wrap you in the warmth that you deserve when all your physical beauty is gone. Look for a relationship that will meet your needs today, tomorrow and for years to come.

Your assignment for today is to write yourself a letter and tell yourself what you deserve, so when Mr. Wrong comes, you will have a reminder that you deserve better.

DAY 25
A New Attitude
Setting your Agenda

Once you know that you deserve the love you desire, most of the battle is won. The next step is opening up and letting it come in. Your new agenda should be living life in love and hope. You know the questions you should ask before you get involved. Your Sphere of Influence is lined up to keep you honest. There's a clear and precise vision of what you want and what you need. Your personally defined profile will point you in the right direction on your search. The work that you have previously competed has made you keenly aware of the past, but it's not holding you hostage. You've looked at your relationship patterns and now you have the tools to seek the truth. Your Deal Breakers are at the forefront of your mind and when you find deception you know how to put your flashers on, pull over and turn around. Most importantly, you know what you deserve and you're ready to receive it and graciously give the same to your partner. Now it's time to learn how to put all these pieces together.

As discussed before, some things on your agenda are comprisable and others are not. Your new agenda is your own happiness and your measurement of success. Happiness is your highest priority. Your main objective is to be aware of who you are, what you want and the steps necessary to get to your birthright, which is to be blissfully happy and whole. That does not mean that you won't face disappointment, hurt feelings and a few dark and depressing days. It means your desire is to be happy and not settle for less than what you deserve.

A major step in your breakthrough is positioning yourself to attract romantic love but more importantly to love yourself until that love comes. If it is your heart's desire to have a family and you meet a guy/girl who is almost perfect for you, but he/she does not share your desire for a family, it may be difficult but you may have to bless him/her and send them on to a love that's right for them. It may be necessary to move on, if you know that there will always be a yearning in your heart for children and the two of you cannot reconcile this issue, you will have to decide who's happiness is more important. Don't allow your dreams to be sidetracked. Don't spend your time thinking that you can change him/her or manipulate, lie, cheat or be deceptive to get what you want. It takes a wise and courageous person to admit to themselves that the person that makes their heart sing cannot give them the things that will make them happy. They may be able to provide some short-term pleasure, but it may be short lived and shrouded in bad consequences. Be true to yourself and think of your long-term happiness. Give yourself permission to want what you want and know that you deserve it. But also be willing to step aside if a potential partner does not work out, so they can get what they want and deserve. Remember, there's no one like you and you deserve happiness.

In the same vein, if loyalty and fidelity are important to you, be willing to insist on it or be ready to move on. If you find an almost perfect person that's a swinger and he/she loves you but it's clear that for him/her to be happy he/she must have multiple partners, then you need to move on or proceed with extreme caution. If you know that the swinger's lifestyle isn't what you can personally live with, then you have to make a decision for your own happiness. You have to love yourself enough to bless this person and send them on their way. It's very hard to leave but in some cases, it's much harder to stay.

With your new agenda you are holding a place for a new love, support and commitment. You are clear on what you want and what you need. Your goals and mission are clear. If it takes a little while don't despair, the "good love" you find will be worth the wait. If you compromise too soon, it might mean that you are making a reservation for a room at heartbreak hotel again. Vote for you! Stand for you! Make your agenda the highest priority and chose the right person to help you get there. Whatever you have to accomplish will be that much sweeter with the love of your life by your side. In the lonely moments, work on yourself to become the best you and to achieve your life goals knowing that your best you will carry you into the arms of a deserving and loving partner. Remember the decisions you make about who you chose to love not only affects you, but everyone in your world. I've seen women/men who have chosen to love people who have abused them, abused their children, stolen from them, given them deadly diseases, their family members have been wounded and even killed trying to protect them and many more atrocities that are too numerous to mention. It's so important to understand that while loving your partner, you must also love yourself. If loving him/her means that you put yourself in danger then you don't sufficiently love yourself, because you should love yourself enough to protect yourself from predators, even if you love them. If the relationship takes you backward rather than forward you are not properly loving yourself. Love yourself enough to leave. Love your children and family enough to keep them out of harm's way.

This decision may be heartbreaking. It can cause some tears and you may be forced to pull the cover over your head and weep. But your breakthrough, transformation and your absolute best self are waiting for you on the other side of those emotions and that sense of loss. In that moment you are standing for yourself and making your happiness your highest priority. When you love yourself enough to make difficult decisions and do what is right for your life and longevity, then you are ready for a love that appreciates you and your sacrifices.

Choose wisely, choose you and make sure your agenda is clear. Compromise if he/she wears yellow socks, but don't compromise on your safety, health, freedom and sanity. Your agenda should keep you away from many of the potholes on the road to love if you embrace it, tweak it where necessary, listen to your Sphere of Influence and listen to your instincts. It's your life, your love, and your agenda. Use it wisely. Be mindful that many of the unwise relationship decisions that people make are made because they are lonely. These desperate decisions usually do not end in fulfilling and lasting relationships, so please realize that loneliness should not cause you to make another bad relationship decision that will thwart your progress.

Your Assignment for today is to make a list of the times that you put yourself in physical, emotional or health related danger as a result of your relationship choices.

93

only affects you, but everyone in your world. I've seen women/men who have chosen to love people who have abused them, abused their children, stolen from them, given them deadly diseases, their family members have been wounded and even killed trying to protect them and many more atrocities that are too numerous to mention. It's so important to understand that while loving your partner, you must also love yourself. If loving him/her means that you put yourself in danger then you don't sufficiently love yourself, because you should love yourself enough to protect yourself from predators, even if you love them. If the relationship takes you backward rather than forward you are not properly loving yourself. Love yourself enough to leave. Love your children and family enough to keep them out of harm's way.

This decision may be heartbreaking. It can cause some tears and you may be forced to pull the cover over your head and weep. But your breakthrough, transformation and your absolute best self are waiting for you on the other side of those emotions and that sense of loss. In that moment you are standing for yourself and making your happiness your highest priority. When you love yourself enough to make difficult decisions and do what is right for your life and longevity, then you are ready for a love that appreciates you and your sacrifices.

Choose wisely, choose you and make sure your agenda is clear. Compromise if he/she wears yellow socks, but don't compromise on your safety, health, freedom and sanity. Your agenda should keep you away from many of the potholes on the road to love if you embrace it, tweak it where necessary, listen to your Sphere of Influence and listen to your instincts. It's your life, your love, and your agenda. Use it wisely. Be mindful that many of the unwise relationship decisions that people make are made because they are lonely. These desperate decisions usually do not end in fulfilling and lasting relationships, so please realize that loneliness should not cause you to make another bad relationship decision that will thwart your progress.

Your Assignment for today is to make a list of the times that you put yourself in physical, emotional or health related danger as a result of your relationship choices.

DAY 26
What I really, really want

Most of us think we know what we really, really want. But the decisions we make prove we really, really don't. More often than not, we look for short-term distractions instead of partners that will stand the test of time. Instead of the man/woman that will provide the long-term love, support, and nourishment, we choose the flavor of the week, the hot girl, the bad boy, the person that will satisfy our desires temporarily, but not lead us toward our long-term relationship goals.

I've asked almost every divorced person I know this question, "On your wedding day, did you believe with all your heart that this marriage would last?" At least thirty percent of people I asked said no, they didn't think it would go "till death do you part," but they were hopeful. They thought that being married would change their spouse. They hoped that their spouse would change this habit or that habit. Or that if they loved their partner enough, that it would work itself out. And because most of these people chose to ignore what they knew in their hearts, they found themselves divorced, broken-hearted, in financial ruins, and trying to pick themselves up for the sake of their children. In the process some had been battered, others have various diseases. Now they know that the heartbreak could have been avoided by just admitting to themselves that they knew what they knew. Be clear that a marriage license will not change a person's character.

Be truthful with yourself, because in most instances the only person you are fooling is yourself. Another example from my own life is when I learned this lesson. I met a guy that seemed great, but there was something that was really nagging at me. I couldn't put my finger on it, but my intuition signaled that something was not quite right. There was nothing on the surface. He was courteous, accomplished and

95

very handsome. But for some reason I could never completely relax around him. As the relationship progressed I set up a double date so I could introduce him to a member of my Sphere of Influence. When we got a chance to talk, my friend thought there was something a little too smooth about him. In the Internet age, I ran as much information as I could gather through several search engines and discovered that he had a large unpaid child support bill. My best friend told me that it didn't concern me, because I didn't plan to have children. But the fact that he had not paid child support was a testament to his character. He was not broke, unemployed or ill. He was quite successful, which meant that this child support issue was a choice, not the result of financial devastation, illness or lack.

I kept my eyes and ears open, not sure if this one thing should be a Deal Breaker. After all, he was attentive, adventuresome and very easy on the eyes. When I asked if he saw his children often, he said no their mom had remarried. This made me even more concerned, because his demeanor told me it was a closed subject. But it didn't make sense because her marriage and his children were two different things. I understand that divorce and co-parenting is difficult even in the best of circumstances, but to not see your children and not participate in their support led me to question his judgment, commitment and his character.

Since the jury was still out on him, I went to my list of questions to see if his answers were compatible with the partner I wanted. One of the questions I asked him was "what he thought the woman's role was in a relationship?" His reply was "to do what I say." At first I started to laugh, thinking he was joking, and then I noticed his expression and countenance was completely serious. Being the person I am with my ideology and upbringing, I knew this was a Deal Breaker for me. We had several long conversations and I discovered his worldview and mine were in direct opposition to each other. I could not, nor did I want to be the woman he wanted. It was time to bless him and send him on his way.

A couple of my friends tried to tell me that I was crazy because he was such a good catch. He was a part of the 10% club, owning a successful business with the houses, cars and toys to show for it. However, I knew what I really wanted was a relationship that was a partnership, based on mutual trust and respect. I'm not the "do as I say" kind of a girl. I wanted someone who valued my opinion and my intellect.

The bottom line is that we have to look at the facts as they are and not interject our own romantic notations and fairy tales into the situation. The question has to be asked, "What am I choosing to overlook?" I've seen women/men overlook a multitude of sin and lie to themselves, saying, "I didn't know" when they chose either consciously or unconsciously to not see the obvious. They chose to look over affairs, drinking problems, gambling problems, domestic violence issues, credit issues, prison records and Deal Breakers of every kind.

There is an old adage that says, "Hindsight is 20/20." The goal is to have your love vision be 20/20, not only in hindsight but from the beginning. This is accomplished by reading the signs, seeing what's there instead of the smoke and mirrors. This isn't to say that any potential partner will be without flaws. The point is to see the flaws, accept the ones that are acceptable and don't go into a relationship pretending the flaws don't exist and wishing that they will magically disappear just because he/she put a ring on it.

I understand that sometimes potential partners carefully cover their flaws and purposely mislead you. There will always be some of that, but it's your job to ask the right questions, read the signs, do the research, recognize the truth and know when you are being told what you want to hear rather than the truth.

If two people are not on the same page it can be devastating to the relationship. The key here is to know what you want, be able to clearly express it and be able to move on if the basic relationship fundamentals don't match. It's imperative that you know who you are, what you want, what is comprisable, and what isn't. The time for the "hope it works out" strategy is long gone. Of course there's never a guarantee that a relationship will work out in the long run. However, if you go into a relationship deceptively or with a hidden agenda, then the odds of the relationship failing greatly increases.

Please resist the temptation to settle for Mr./Ms. Right Now instead of Mr./Ms. Right. When you clearly see a person for who they truly are, rather than a well-crafted facade created for the purpose of deception, don't bury your head in the sand. See the signs and govern yourself accordingly. If the sign says STOP, then stop. If it says dangerous curve, slow down and get out of danger. Don't fool yourself into thinking you can change him/her; accept what is in front of your eyes. The only thing that can change a man or woman is their desire to change.

At one time in my life I may have tried to make things work with "Mr. Do as I Say." On the surface he was generous, kind, successful and thoughtful. But there was something brewing just beneath the surface, I didn't know what it was but my intuition warned me and I blessed him and sent him on. Years later I met his ex wife's sister. She told me that he had been very controlling and abusive to her sister. At that point I was glad I knew what I really wanted and chose to bless and release the relationship.

Wait until Mr./Ms. Right comes and learn how to occupy the restlessness in you until your treasure is revealed. Enjoy your life until you find a long-term mate that you know will be worth waiting for. Rather than settling for some seat filler for right now. Spend your time having big fun and learning to empower yourself. Find new and creative ways to love yourself, because when the time is right you are going to have to teach Mr./Ms. Right how to love you and treat you. Nourish your friendships and familial relationships, practice loving the people in your life and develop a support system that tells you the truth, strengthens you and pushes you toward your greatness. Try new things. You might even be surprised to find the right person while you are out doing the things you love. Wouldn't it be great to find someone who loves to do the same things you love to do? Until then, know what you really, really want.

Your assignment for today is to write your story about discovering what you thought you wanted and how you discovered that it was wrong for you.

DAY 27
Communicating
Standing in your truth

When you make a conscious decision to be different, the universe will challenge you to make sure you mean what you say. Over the last several weeks you've learned a lot about yourself, your family patterns, and your choice in men/women. Knowledge is power and this knowledge will help you be better and choose better. Most of the decisions you made up to this point have been unconscious, but now you are conscious and your skills have been sharpened.

Prior to this point, you probably haven't taken the time to really think your relationships through carefully and develop the strategy for finding a good relationship. Most of the relationship decisions were probably based on attraction rather than strategy. For many the strategy up to this point was to "hope" that it would work out. In some cases that strategy may have been successful but most of the time it is not. For a relationship to work, both people have to work at it and they both have to want to arrive at the same destination. Therefore, you have to know who you are and what you want in order to find someone who is going in the same direction. The key to success here is communication.

The universe will test you and you will probably get calls from some of your exes or some good looking guy or girl with an incompatible worldview. A potential partner may arrive in your life with a contradictory agenda to see whether or not you are serious in your conviction to find "good love". You will have to make some decisions and I pray you recognize the decoy and make a decision to do what is best for you. However, if you find yourself on a one-way street going the wrong direction, find a safe place to turn around and analyze how you got there.

Healthy relationships are about balance, compromise, communication and meeting each other's needs.

If one person is getting all their needs met and the other is being sucked dry, this imbalance is going to lead to a situation where one person is happy and the other is malnourished and seeking nourishment and support from a source other than the confines of the relationship. Healthy relationships are not about manipulating, making your partner feel guilty, or holding sex hostage to get what you want.

Healthy relationships are about effectively communicating and getting on the same page and enjoying and loving each other along the journey. The best way to get what you want is to be able to openly and honestly articulate what you want to your partner and listen to their wants and needs.

I've seen so many women who think that their man should be able to figure out what they want and supply their every need. That's simply not the case. Most men I know are not mind readers and when they ask, "what's wrong" it's because they simply don't know. I believe the reason so many women respond "nothing" is because they don't have the language to describe what they're feeling. If this is true for you, once you realize that your needs are not being met, don't pout and say nothing is wrong. Clearly and calmly articulate what the problem is and how it makes you feel.

This is a problem I see with women especially. They seem to think that their men should automatically and magically know what they want and need without it being adequately articulated. Don't assume he/she should know. Have the necessary conversation to get the relationship back on track. Use your words. Ask for what you want. Express your upset clearly and if you don't have the words immediately at your disposal, let your partner know that "yes" something is wrong, but you need a little time to gather your thoughts and examine your emotions so that you can state your feelings in a clear and concise way. When you have had time to gather your thoughts express what is wrong in a way that he/she will understand and the two of you can work toward a solution. Provide examples of where things have gone wrong and what your partner can do to correct them, as well as nourish and support you.

And be willing to do your part to meet your partner half way. Stay on topic and do not use your upset as an opportunity to verbally abuse your partner or vent about things that happened ten years ago unless the problem is continuous and your present upset is just an example of the same issue. Remember, it takes two to make it and it takes two to break it.

When you are trying to communicate with your partner, don't make the conversation a screaming match. If you are angry at the time, take some time to calm yourself so you can be heard and a solution can be worked-out. Give your partner the opportunity to make things right. Additionally, hear his/her complaints and do what you need to do to make sure that everyone in the relationship gets their needs met. If both people are happy and content it's a win-win situation. If after the conversation you discover that you two are not on the same page then try to exhaust all of your options and keep the lines of communication open. Try to correct the problems and if you need therapy, get it. But don't continue to suffer. If after you have tried everything and you have no more options, then it might be time to make a decision to go or to stay. Only you can decide what answer is best for you.

The "New" you is going to work very hard at expressing the feelings, emotions, upsets, do, don'ts and disappointments in a way that a partner can hear it, understand it and chose to help make it right or decide that they don't have the skills or desire to make it right. Before you consider starting a new relationship make sure you are CLEAR that you know what you want. Make sure your Deal Breakers are clear, your needs are clear and your expectations are clear and that you can easily articulate what you want, need and expect of your partner.

One way to avoid having your needs ignored is to be brutally honest with yourself. Be strong enough to hear what is being said rather than what you want to hear. If he/she says I love you and I want to be with you, but he/she is constantly out with their friends and breaking dates with you, there is a serious contradiction between his/her words and deeds. If your birthdays and special dates are not acknowledged and you're treated as a second thought rather than a priority, then you have to hear what is being said. If there is a disconnect between your partners words and deeds area common occurrence, then you need to realize that you are being lied to. If your partner's words and the deeds are not matching up, hear and see the deeds. If I told you I loved you and then punched you in the stomach, I pray that sooner or later you would learn to move out of arm's reach, because my punching you is anything but loving. Every attempt has to be made to get on the same page and make sure that what you hear him/her saying is verified by his/her actions.

Communication is the key to making all things work. You should communicate your goals and what type of relationship you want. If one partner wants an open relationship while the other wants complete loyalty and fidelity, that creates a problem that, will be difficult to compromise on. Another thing that might be difficult to compromise on is whether or not to have a family. There are very few things that couples absolutely have to agree on, but there are a few. Communication is a must here.

Another major issue that couples should be clear on is money. How will family money be handled? Will the finances be separate? Will all the money be put in one pot and everyone have access to it? Will the bills be divided by percentage of income or down the middle? Will one partner make it all and the other spend it all? Will there be an investment plan? Does one partner believe in paying bills on time and the other believe that we only live once so let's live it up and worry about credit and retirement when we are sixty-five? These are real life issues that can cause havoc in a relationship. You must be willing to openly discuss these issues and have some understanding of what each partner wants before you consider a long-term relationship.

Another issue that's very important to the success of the relationship is how children, if any, will be raised. What will discipline look like? Will there be discipline? Parents being on the same page about these issues is crucial to the success of children. Communicating your ideology will make these subjects much easier to navigate.

While there will be all kinds of hiccups along the way, these things will be easier to survive if there's a clear understanding from the beginning.

102

It's better that these subjects come to the forefront earlier rather than later. Of course, the right time to discuss these things isn't on the first date but certainly before too many emotions are vested in the relationship. It's a matter of living in integrity and putting your cards out on the table for a prospective partner to see and if he/she does not like what's in your hand, then it's time to bless him/her and allow them to move on so you can be one step closer to the person that's an almost perfect complement.

If you learn to bless and release those who are obvious mismatches then you can focus on your almost perfect match. If they are good people but not good partner material, keep them as friends.

Another, great thing my mom used to tell me is "a bird and a fish can fall in love, but where are they going to live?" Sometimes the passion and the attraction are there but how do you find a common place to live and thrive?

Your assignment is to answer the questions above and to look over your relationships and pinpoint places and times when good communication would have saved you from heartbreak.

DAY 28
The Choice
To have or to Let go

The lyrics of an old song blues song by Betty Wright that says, "Having a piece of man is better than having no man." Whenever I hear the song played on some of the oldies stations it always gives me pause because I know that the mentality of so many people is to have someone, even if it's the wrong person. Some people believe that it's better to be coupled inappropriately than to be alone. It's a decision that every man/woman has to decide for themselves. The questions I always ask when this situation arise are:

- Do you want to invest time, energy and emotions in someone who you know is wrong for you?
- Do you settle for a relationship where you know you will most likely not get your needs met?
- Is that relationship worth holding on to if, the other option is being alone?

The question that must be answered is, if faced with the possibility of being alone do you settle for any seat filler that comes along or do you say no to him/her and take the risk of being alone? Will you be able to make peace with the seat filler and try to be content? And, are you willing to risk Mr./Ms. Right coming along and not being available because you are attached to Mr./Ms. Wrong. What will your answer be? And on the other hand, how long can you be single before you settle?

Sometimes out of desperation any warm body will do, just for companionship and adult conversation. Can you admit that some of the heartbreak you've experienced was a result of your deliberate choices to accept Mr./Ms. Wrong and pretend that it was Mr./Ms. Right? I would venture to guess that in many instances you knew what you were accepting into your life was not what you needed. These are questions that most people will have to answer as you weed through possibilities until you find the right person to compliment you.

104

There will be periods of time when you are single. How will you fill those days, weeks, months or maybe years? Will you seek a Mr./Ms. Right Now? Will you take Mr./Ms. Wrong and try to change him/her into Mr./Ms. Right? That is of course possible, some people just need a little help and encouragement, and with time they may actually become your Mr./Ms. Right. If you refuse Mr./Ms. Wrong, Mr./Ms. Right Now and Mr./Ms. fixer-upper what do you do in the meantime? How will you handle the birthdays, Christmases, company picnics, weddings and lonely nights? What is your plan of action?

Bear in mind that this single and alone time might be exactly what you need to get in touch with your past and where you want to go from here. Being single can have its benefits if you use the time properly. It can be a growing experience and a fact-finding expedition into who you are and what you want. It can be a time of making peace with who you are and who you hope to become. It can be a time for healing the past wounds and breaking restrictive patterns and worldviews that have hindered your relationships in the past.

This single period can be anything you want it to be. You can spend it depressed and miserable or you can make it an adventure to discover your own greatness. You have to answer the question of having and holding or letting go. Everyone has a different pain threshold and regardless of how much the people around you love you, these decisions are yours alone to make.

You will have to live with the decisions you make and the consequences that develop as a result. What if you choose a seat filler and that relationship resulted in a child? Could you make that situation work for the rest of your life in order to parent your child? Ask yourself, is it okay to accept 10%, 20%, and 30% of what you need? At what point do you stand for yourself and demand more out of your relationships? And more importantly, when do you demand more from yourself? Try not to settle for something that you wouldn't want your daughter or son to settle for, because your example is what your child will follow. Demand the best for yourself, and then you can be the person who will one day teach your children how to demand the best for themselves as well.

There are a few cautions that I would hope you would consider. It's hard to offer Mr./Ms. Right a seat when someone else is already sitting there. If you find someone and you have a seat filler do you become a cheater, or live without authenticity?

Secondly you have to decide if you are willing to give up a part of yourself to someone who may not deserve it or appreciate it. This may affect your self-esteem and lead you to heartbreak, yet again. You must decide if it's worth it to find yourself in the same place again.

Thirdly, you have to ask yourself if you are trying to continue the same addictive patterns that have brought you to this place. Sometimes you can be addicted to ill treatment and bad relationships because it helps to reinforce poor self-esteem, feelings of inadequacy and perpetual heartbreak, the consummate victim.

You have to make hard decisions. Do you want to couple differently? Or in hard or single times will you resort to your old relationship patterns? Tell yourself the truth, even if it's painful. You cannot keep beating a dead horse, while expecting it to win the Kentucky Derby. At some point you have to realize that it's dead and needs to be buried. It's time to move on unapologetically to a fulfilling relationship that supports you in fulfilling your goals.

I worked with a beautiful young woman who was just as smart as she was pretty. She started dating a young man when she was in high school. Her parents did not like this young man. They tried everything to get her to end this relationship, but the more they pressed her to end it the more she clung to him.

As soon as she graduated and turned 18 she married him. She was determined to prove her parents wrong. It did not take her long until she realized that her parents were right but she was determined not to show it. He ended up going to prison and she said she was going to stand by him for better or for worse like her vows said. She drove a couple of hundred miles twice per month to see him.

After almost two years he came out of prison angrier than when he went in. She was afraid to ask for help or call the police because he was on probation and she didn't want to see him sent to jail again. She was bruised and battered sometimes almost beyond recognition. It took four years for her to wake up, but by then she was left with nothing, living in a shelter and too embarrassed to turn to her parents because of all the nasty things she had said and done to them. She was left wondering where her youth and her life went. Her pride caused her to stay in a relationship that she should have gotten out of. Instead of trying to prove her parents wrong, she should have tried to prove was her own worth. Hopefully your consequences will never be this drastic but there are consequences for everything you do, even choosing to hold on when you know you should let go.

Your assignment for today is to list the times that you held on when you should have let go.

DAY 29
Counting the Cost

Each Relationship has an associated cost. The bad relationships are very costly. When you look back on the cost and the lost time associated with two, five, ten, or even twenty years of bad relationships, what has been the collateral damage? How much further along would you have been in your career, financial plans, family harmony and social obligations if you had realized or spoken your regret and let that relationship pass you by? Where do you think you would be now? What has been the cost of these bad relationships on you, your psyche, your self-esteem, your children, your family, your career, or finances? Can you put a price on what it cost you monetarily, emotionally, socially or in family relationships?

I know some great things like beautiful children come from bad relationships, but what has been the effect of a difficult home life on those children? More importantly, how much more will it cost you if you continue the pattern for another five years, ten or twenty years? Will your children lose respect for you? Will you be passed over for promotions, because your spouse always gets drunk and gets inappropriate at your work functions? It is unfortunate but bad relationships affect all aspects of your life. And only you get to decide if the price worth it?

I've seen lives lost due to bad relationships, I've seen fortunes lost because of bad relationships, I've seen children maimed and abused because of bad relationships and I've seen families torn apart by one member's coupling choice. We all see the disasters unfold on the local network news and we are lulled into thinking that the murder suicides, child abuse and molestations happen to other people, but they can happen to anyone who does not read the signs, see what's in plain view or make relationship choices from a healthy, calculate and objective place. When is the cost too much for you? What are you willing to lose as a result of your relationship choices? What has been the cost of these bad relationships on you, your psyche, your self-esteem, your children, your family, your career, or finances? Did it cost you monetarily, emotionally, socially or in family relationships?

Your assignment for today is to calculate the cost of all your bad relations. How much did it cost you in

- Time
- Money
- Education
- Youth
- Child Support
- Career Advancement
- Social Standing
- Respect from your children
- Family Relations and Friendships

Was the relationship worth it?

109

Every relationship functions differently based on the partner's wants, needs and desires. Relationships are fluid and ever changing as the people in them are constantly changing. However, there are some basic relationship styles that most relationships fall into. They are: Parent-Child, Child-Child, and Adult-Adult. Under each of these relationship types are several different decrees and sub categories that fall under each category. For the sake of simplicity, I will only introduce the basic framework for each. It's important to determine what type of relationship style fits you and your partner best.

Parent-Child Relationship

Just as it states, in the relationship there is a partner in charge who is the parent. This is the person who makes the rules, sets the relationship parameters and who will usually control the finances and every aspect of the relationship. What the parent says goes and there is little debate. The parent makes the decisions and issues directives that must be followed. The Child is the partner who follows the orders. They do as they're told or they suffer the repercussions as most children do. The partners are not equal and equality is not the goal in this type of relationship. This was the relationship style of my ex-boyfriend, "Mr. do as I tell you," believed in. There's a leader and a follower. The parent gets his/her needs met and the child is there to fulfill the needs of the parent. The child gets their needs meet as long as there is compliance to the parent's directives.

Usually it's the husband that's the parent and the wife, who plays the role of the child. The child, is dependent upon the parent for financial support and instructions. The child usually does as they're told until they are absolutely sick of being controlled. The child wants to grow up and when that time comes, the child begins to act out, rebel and become sneaky, at which point the parent attempts to tighten the reins to control the rebellious child. This relationship style works for some people. I've seen the Parent-Child relationships style be effective when both parties are committed to the roles they play. Or if one partner does not want any responsibility in the relationship, they may want to be taken care of and choose to play the child's role to be responsibility-free. In some cases, the Child is a master manipulator and can get anything from the parent. Other times the Child makes the Parent think they are the Parent when in actuality the Child is back stage pulling the strings.

You will often find the Parent-Child style in very religious families. The man is the head of the house and makes the decisions for the relationship. It can be successful especially if the parent is a good provider and takes care of all the child's needs. However, this style can also foster an abusive environment because in reality every parent reserves the right to discipline their child the way he/she sees fit.

Child-Child Relationships

This relationship style is quite different from the Parent-Child Relationship style. No one is in charge and both partners act like children. There is no plan of how to navigate long-term challenges or relationship up and downs. The relationship is about today and how I feel today. There are no rules the partners stay together as long as it's fun. The partners are free spirited and lively. There are no regulations or relationship guidelines. It's all about fun, big fun and forget about responsibility. In this category relationships can be disposable. You stay as long as it meets your needs, or until the excitement wears off. When the relationship gets boring or too serious, then the children begin to look for new toys (relationships). They handle life's challenges by throwing temper tantrums and walking out. People who believe in this relationship style don't believe their lives should change as a result of being in a committed relationship. They believe they should still be able to go out and have fun without any repercussions. The Child-Child relationship style is devoid of responsibility and people who operate in this style are usually those that fear commitment or being tied down or controlled. They love their partners but can be transient especially if they feel they are being overwhelmed by their partner's needs and expectations. The children can also be very financially immature, spending on whatever the child wants at the time, without concern for the family budget or future credit problems. This relationship style is usually practiced by younger couples, but normally at some point someone grows up and tries to switch relationship styles. One of the children will normally become disillusioned of being a child in an adult's body so they try to grow up and become responsible. One of the children will usually try to parent the other and sometimes that may be successful as long as the child is not denied too much fun. Sometimes both partners will grow up and form one of the other categories or they will move on. The issues usually become very apparent when a baby in brought into the union and someone is forced to be a real adult. One child will grow up and demand that the partner grow up and share in the responsibility of a growing family. The child-partner will then decide to grow up and become responsible or run for the hills, leaving their partner to take care of a baby alone. As long as there aren't too many restrictions or obligations placed on the child, this relationship can be fun, exciting and fulfilling. This style of relationship is common for the very young and also for some divorced people who have raised their families and are retired and looking for excitement from second or third marriages.

Adult-Adult Relationships

The Adult-Adult relationship style is based on equal partners, where each partner is respected and honored for their strengths. There's usually a pre-determined division of duties and financial responsibilities. The roles are not static, they change based on the needs of the relationship. Each partner is considered and both people consult together to make decisions for the unit. It's a relationship that requires dialogue, compromise and commitment. There's usually a plan in place concerning role expectations, finances, retirement, social commitments, children, Deal Breakers and both partners work together to make sure that they achieve their goals as a family. The contract is often renegotiated at various stages of their lives together. Oftentimes a relationship will start out in another style and morph into the Adult-Adult style.

112

As partners began to mature they sometime begin to want to interact with an adult. When children are introduced into the relationship many couples will revise how their relationship functions.

Every couple is free to develop the relationship style that fits them best. You have to decide which style speaks to your wants and needs. Each style has its advantages, you just have to know where your relationship desires will flourish. The caution is to make a choice of the style you want and not be bullied into one or another. Before you make a long-term commitment with someone make sure you know a little about what their relationship style is and whether their choice will meet your needs now and in the future.

Finding the right style of relationship is very important. If you know you are very outspoken and opinionated and you chose a partner that sub-scribes to a Parent-Child relationship style where you are the child and placed in a subservient role, then that's major TROUBLE. Or you can find yourself the parent of an adult child, which can be very frustrating. Remember, start off the way you plan to finish. Please don't think you can change a child into an adult or a parent into an adult. Observe what is really there and decide if you can live with it.

Your assignment for today is to identify the relationship styles that you've had in the past and decide if you want the same styles in your future relationships.

DAY 31
Hitting the reset button

When you have followed the steps outlined in *Break-up Break Through* and you have found someone who you believed met your relationship criteria, but over time you have discovered this relationship isn't a good match after all, you then have to learn how to press the reset button. The first thing that you must do is to evaluate what went wrong. What did you overlook or choose not to see? Did your partner present his representative and you did not see the real character until it was too late? Whatever the reason, make sure you get the lesson from the relationship so you don't make the same mistake again.

The next step is to leave the relationship with some dignity. Even though it can be painful, ending a relationship has it rewards. It can give you the opportunity to reevaluate what you want, what you need, your list of questions, and what your Deal Breakers are. During this period you can concentrate on you and pull your energy inward. You can get a clear and concise reading on the adjustments you need to make to have a more successful relationship next time. You will have to learn to bless a relationship and move on once you are clear that it's not what you need.

Try to make a peaceable break. It could be that this is the right person, but not the right time. He/she may not be ready for the type of relationship you want and need right now, but with the lines of communication open he/she may be ready a year from now. If you leave the relationship in a dignified manner it can allow for a future friendship and useful dialogue as to how things went wrong. Being able to amicably dialogue with an ex can provide valuable insights to your blind spots that only an intimate partner would be able to reveal. Oftentimes, you don't get to find out what went wrong from his/her perspective and this is very valuable information that can help you discover who you are in a relationship, because your perception could be

114

slightly off. Often you think you are making one impression, but your partner may experience something different. The ex conversations can provide clarity and reveal how potential partners perceive you. You can learn a lot about your relationship styling's by learning to leave a relationship under good terms. I'm not saying that you should set out to make you ex your best friend, but leaving the relationship in a way that allows you to have a cordial conversation or greet each other on the street is a plus.

Knowing how to leave a relationship with dignity is very much a learned skilled. In the midst of a break-up, emotions and tempers are elevated and when you are angry being amicable or cordial are not on your radar. Sometimes the relationship ending has left you hurt and you want to express your hurt by inflicting your own brand of hurt and pain on your ex-partner. But think of it as if you're leaving a job. Even though the job may have been horrible and the management were imbeciles, you still would want to leave the job in a way that you feel could confident in asking for a good reference. It may not have been a good fit but that doesn't mean you need to throw a tantrum and have to be escorted out in handcuffs by security.

Think of leaving a relationship in the same vein. It did not turn out the way you thought it would, but you learned something, you got some experience. You put yourself out there and made the effort to make it work. The experience you gathered can now go on your love resume. Sometimes the problem is that you stayed much longer than you should have and you began to feel resentful, unappreciated, ashamed and scared of your options if you left. In reality, the decision is yours and has always been yours. You decide to go and if you should stay.

The majority of relationships' break-ups are not cordial. Oftentimes people feel that if the relationship is flawed or damaged that they have to act out horribly to leave it. Some couples feel that they can't break up unless they fight and break things and make a mockery of the weeks, months or years they spent together. It's not necessary to have a big loud break-up and make a spectacle for the neighbors. You simply must admit that you know it's time to go. Have the necessary conversations and try to agree to an amicable split.

It's like when you're driving in an area that isn't familiar to you and you realize you are getting into some dangerous territory. The scenery is changing and you feel uneasy. You finally admit to yourself that you are lost and the route you are on will not get you to your destination safely. If you continue traveling the same direction, you may get car-jacked or need a police escort to get you out of it. My experience has been that it's best to find some place to turn around, pull out your GPS or ask for directions.

With everything that you have learned in Break-up Breakthrough you have the tools necessary to make the adjustments in your program to get a better relationship next time. You've learned the questions to ask, what to look out for and when to make your exit. You get a chance to review what your Sphere of Influence had to say. Right now you are in the perfect place, even though it may not feel that way. Ending a relationship helps you to gather your emotions and improve your relationship road map.

Do not cast blame; take full responsibility. It was a mutual decision to start the relationship and you have to admit that there was something in you that needs healing that attracted you to another person that's broken and in need of healing. If you can admit your part and talk to your ex. Maybe you both can find the places where you are both honest and help each other to make better decisions.

Your assignment is to chronicle the ways in which you have broken up with partners in the past and decide if your behavior was fruitful.

Most people have the desire to couple, it's a natural part of life. Sometimes it's necessary to make sure that the person you have chosen to couple with is coupling with you for the qualities you bring to the table rather than the resources that you have. At various stages of life these question will be more pertinent than at other times. If you are a broke college student coupling with another broke college student then there are no real resources to protect. But it's much different if you are a trust fund baby and everyone knows it. Or if you have been very successful in business and you have all the shiny new toys and cash to prove it. That isn't to say that everyone who seeks you out is after your money, but there may be a few bad apples in the potential partner pool. It's up to you to ascertain the motives of possible mates. Your Sphere of Influence can certainly be helpful on this one.

I learned a huge life lesson from the mother of my ex-boyfriend. She told me that her prayer for her sons when it came to finding the appropriate spouse was "to find someone who came to share with them not to take from them." There's a lot of wisdom in her words. This concept of sharing versus taking is one that should be forever on your mind when considering a relationship. It was interesting to me because most parents want their children to find someone who is successful, aesthetically beautiful, and rich or so many other adjectives. But she wanted someone for her sons that came to share rather than to take. I found this fascinating. I thought about my relationships in a new way, categorizing them as sharing or taking. I sat down and looked at my relationships from this perspective and it was eye opening. I invite you to do the same.

If there's someone you are considering coupling with and they want to come into your life and share your life's journey, time and resources, but bring some contributions to the table that's a great find. If however you find someone that's coming into your life to take

117

whatever they can get their hands on, then that's another thing altogether. I would advise you to run from this person as fast as you can. Someone who is coming to sap your resources, take what they can get and misuse your love isn't a partner that will be long-term. Their intention may be to get while the getting is good. Then move on to the next person with deep pockets. Unless you are going into the situation with eyes wide open and you don't mind being taken advantage of, then I would advise you to beware.

There are so many people who are looking to succeed and move up by coupling with someone who can finance their habits and support their lifestyles. Usually there is no love to offer. They come with refurbished armor and surgically altered facades to take rather than to share. Make sure you can tell the difference between a sharer and a taker. One way to tell the difference is to listen to your instincts and be completely honest with yourself. Compare their words to their deeds. Have open, honest discussions and investigate, investigate, investigate. Run them by your Sphere of Influence and ask the questions on your list and listen for the truth.

Being that life is cyclical sometimes things are great and money is flowing like water, while other times it may be difficult to get ends to meet. Sometimes the economy is good other times not so much. If you have a sharer in your life, then the two of you can find a way to work together to be successful. If you have a taker as a partner then you might be left high and dry for the next Black American Express Card.

I was working with a gentleman in his fifties and he began to tell me about this beautiful young 28 year old that was in love with him. My antenna went up immediately, but not because that couldn't happen. There are plenty of younger women that like older men and some older men are in great shape and have the looks and stamina of a thirty year old. But the question of coming to take rather than to share always needs to be a consideration. He is an attractive, well-educated and established businessman with a wealth of resources, social clout and contacts. He is a very nice man and it wouldn't be out of the question for a young woman over twenty-five years his junior to fall for him. But one

118

would have to wonder, if she loved him or his resources?

When I asked the question, "Do you think she would love you if you worked for UPS and drove a 15 year old Toyota?" He was appalled by the question and taken aback that I asked it. He looked at me as if I'd grown a second head on my shoulders. It was not something he wanted to consider, but I knew the question was important because in life, things change and when they do you need to know who is in your corner and who is not. People lose fortunes; health and life can change at a moment's notice. You don't want to invest your time, resources and emotions with someone who is only with you because of what you can provide. If he/she would love you regardless of your resources or lack thereof and is with you for better or worse, then congratulations are in order. If he/she is there to take and is only with you while the getting is good, then I would say it's time to make some critical decisions.

A couple weeks later, he told me that he'd asked some of the crucial questions that I provided for him and did a little investigation on his own. The results were not good, and they had parted ways. The discussion was fruitful and eye opening for him. It seems like he would have been intelligent enough to ask the questions on his own, but he did what most of us do. He accepted her on face value, because he enjoyed the attention.

You don't want to assume that everyone is after you for your resources, but you do want to question the possibility. There are partners out there looking for you who don't care what you have. The value in the relationship for them is the person you are and how you make them feel. You'll find them if you don't lead with your resources. If you are making it rain in the nightclubs, of course that's going to attract a certain kind of attention. But if you play down your resources and play up the real you and let your personality shine, it will be more likely that you'll find someone who is coming to share rather than to take.

A colleague of mine was a very successful business owner until he lost almost everything during the economic crisis. He and his wife had to downsize everything. They moved from a grand 6000 square foot home

119

into a two bedroom townhouse. Things were looking very bleak, but he said it was one of the greatest times of his life because he realized how much his wife really loved him. He had been afraid that she would leave him, because he thought he didn't have anything to offer. But she assured him that she was not going anywhere. She stood by him, encouraged him and told him that she never wanted all those things, she only wanted him. They worked together and found ways to survive. It took a couple of years, but they came back stronger and are once again successful and more in love than ever.

Most of the time partners/spouses are in relationships because they love each other and I believe that to be the rule rather than the exception. But there are people who are looking for your resources, not what you personally have to offer, so be aware. You have the tools to figure out which is which.

Your assignment for today is to identify the "sharers" and "takers" in your life and relationships.

DAY 33
Normal or Not

Sometimes we have an idea in our mind of what a mate should or shouldn't be. Sometimes those ideas aren't realistic. Part of the problem is being unrealistic about what relationships are and what a healthy one looks like. For reality's sake it might be necessary to give up on some of the fantasies you have. If you are looking for daddy in every man you meet, you may need to realize that you knew daddy in the role of father, not as the role of husband. Those two roles are completely different. It's very possible that daddy could have been an excellent daddy, but a horrible husband. Additionally, the roles of men and women are quite different than they were fifty years ago or even twenty years ago. As the roles evolve, new rules and expectations must also emerge. So let's see if we can decipher what normal is and is not for a modern day relationship.

It's normal for a couple to have disagreements. Both people bring their different worldviews, expectations, family life, culture and over the weight limit baggage into a relationship. Sometimes these items are like a maze that you have to learn to work your way through, but with mutual respect and communication it's possible to navigate and enjoy the journey and the process. If you are patient and honest, the journey can bring lots of love and laughter.

It's NOT normal however to be abused. Regardless if it's verbal, emotional, physical or sexual, it is not normal and NEVER acceptable. Under all circumstance abuse is wrong and there's no excuse that can ever make it right. If he/she hits you once, there's almost a 100% chance that it will happen again. If abuse is a part of your relationship it's time to RUN. There's NEVER an acceptable reason or excuse for abuse. Shaking, slapping, pushing, shoving, hitting and rape are all forms of abuse and should be Deal Breakers. Additionally, so is emotional, sexual or verbal abuse. These abusive tendencies can escalate into very sinister acts that can have disastrous consequences including death.

121

It's normal for your partner to get on your nerves sometimes. It's normal for him/her to have habits that just annoy you. If you squeeze the toothpaste from the bottom and he/she squeezes it from the top, that's annoying, but it's normal. I actually solved this little issue by buying him his own tube of toothpaste and he can squeeze wherever he likes. I personally have a habit of leaving cabinet doors open when I remove a plate or a glass. It's annoying to my partner, but normal and I'm a little better at it now since it was constantly brought to my attention.

Those little things are not Deal Breakers and should be expected in any relationship. You can learn to pick your battles and not go off the deep end about the small stuff. In the grand scheme of things it doesn't matter if he/she leaves their clothes lying over the chair, if you know without a shadow of a doubt that you are loved and his other flaws are few. But again, it's never normal for your spouse to have habits that can jeopardize the family's health or safety.

If your spouse has gambling debts that have scary characters coming to your door, that isn't normal and you should seek some help. If your spouse spends more time at the gentleman's club than at home, that isn't normal and you should seek some professional help. If your kids tell you that your wife/husband has a couple of kissing cousins that spend the night, when you're not home, that isn't normal and you need to get some help.

It's normal for your spouse to know what you like and dislike and for him/her to attempt to make you happy. It's NOT normal for your spouse to be able to read your mind and know what you want if you refuse to effectively communicate. Communication is always the key, you can't expect your partner to be able to meet your needs if you cannot express them. If you express them and they are ignored that's another thing. When asked, "what's wrong" use your words, express your displeasure and don't leave your partner guessing. If you continue this behavior your partner will eventually stop asking what's wrong or caring. If asking you is not going to produce a response that he/she can address, then why should he/she continue to ask or care?

It's normal for relationships to change. Medical challenges, problems with aging parents or grown children are just a few challenges a relationship may have to endure. It's normal for economic downturns to affect income levels and it's normal for the other spouse to help develop a new plan that's based on normal life changes. Relationships are not often 50/50; sometimes it's 70/30 or even 90/10 because circumstances can change your ability to address and meet your partner's needs. Whatever the percentage, if both partners are 100% committed to the relationship then it's normal. Sometimes if you love your partner you have to step in and take up the slack until he/she is able to bear his/her own load. Life is full of ups and downs and if you are committed to live it together then you have to commit to the roller coaster ride of life. The main thing is to give and take, and hold each other up until each can walk on their own power. You are stronger together than apart. It's NOT normal, however, for one partner to bear all the weight and responsibility and the other to get all the benefits without making a contribution.

Your assignment for today is to decide what your new normal will look like.

DAY 34
Which Flower

As you are wandering through life trying to pick which partner you want to couple with, please be careful not to look for a husband/wife in every man/woman that you meet. So many men and women have one date and they're already planning long-term relationships before they even know if they are dealing with the representative or the authentic person. Dating and meeting new people should be the fun part of the journey. Meeting new people, seeing how they live, finding out about their ideology and ways of being in the world should provide some excitement.

If you are looking at every man/woman you meet as THE ONE, you will probably give off a desperate vibe and scare them away. However, if you approach each person that you meet as if he/she were a new book with interesting facts that you want to read about to see if you like the story, there will be less disappointment and energy loss if it doesn't work. You will miss the storyline, character development and plot if you open the book and only read the first and last page. If you approach dating too hurriedly, you will have to fill in the chapters and subchapters with conjecture that might prove to be detrimental in the long run.

Relax and let the story unfold organically. If you like it, stay around to see what's in the chapters, what the illustrations look like and what the reviews say. Don't try to put a wedding band on anyone during the first date. Take the time to see if he/she is a good fit before you start looking at bridesmaid dresses or tuxedoes.

Approach the getting to know you process as if you are entering school on the first day of first grade. You don't spend your first day of school planning the graduation party or senior prom. There are lessons learned along the way. If you enter first grade with only graduation on your mind you're going to miss all the naps, education, plays,

124

getting your first locker in middle school, getting sent to the principal's office, pranks, practical jokes, and recess in your twelve year matriculation progress. You're going to miss playing an angel in the Christmas play or falling in love with little Suzie or Johnny in the third grade or winning the science fair in fifth grade, the 8th grade prom, making it to the finals in the spelling bee your first bra or chest hair. The journey has a lot of interesting scenery and landmarks on the way, but if you concentrate on the destination only, you'll miss it. There's a lot of learning between first grade and graduation and there's a lot of living, loving and learning between the first date and the wedding date. Let the relationship naturally mature. Think of it as an adventure and if it doesn't lead to a wedding day, you will have had fun along the way and experiences that will serve as the foundation to your relationship education.

Take each step carefully and thoughtfully otherwise you'll skip too many steps and find yourself married to someone you don't know and most importantly someone you don't like, all because you refused to take your time to get to know this person. You will regret it if you don't take the time to read the reviews, investigate and find out that he has five ex-wives and eight children and he was a suspect in the disappearance of wife numbers two and four. Remember, people usually have patterns of behavior, take time to find out what those patterns are and if they will help you grow or stunt your growth. If he/she has been abusive, unfaithful, a gold-digger or cheater in the past then there's a possibility that those behaviors may surface again. You have to take your time and learn about this person. If you don't take the time to see who this person really is, you will have to bear part of the responsibility for anything that happens. In the Internet generation it's very easy to do your research.

If you are too anxious for graduation, it might scare off a guy/girl who would be perfect for you. If you just take the time to let the relationship mature, and take one grade at a time you may get to graduation and graduate with honors.

Another caution is to remember if you have just met this individual and had one or two dates, please don't feel like you have the right to question his/her whereabouts, go through his/her phone or search his/her home.

125

That's too scary and it may make a perfectly good person run for cover. **Don't expect commitment behavior until a commitment has been established.** If you skip the logical progression of steps you can ruin a good relationship before it even starts. Relax, slow down, look around and enjoy. Don't doggedly set your sights on one person. Take a few applications and review some resumes. Settle down and wait for the right pitch before you swing. If your goal is to have fun, the people you meet will observe how much fun you are, you might have admirers come forth and you'll have the task of deciding which flower to pick from many suitors.

Your assignment for today is too look at your previous relationships and determine which ones developed prematurely and why. Decide how you would approach starting a new relationship now.

DAY 35
Quantity vs. Quality

I had the pleasure of working with a very brilliant young woman who felt it was time for her to couple. She was the oldest of four girls. The two youngest sisters were already married and the other sister was soon to be married and was about to have a baby. Her parents were pressing her to get married and she was getting the "you're going to be an old maid" speech.

During one of our conversations, she told me some family members were beginning to question her sexuality. She had goals and she wanted to make her career dreams come to fruition, but this marriage issue was a real sore spot for her. She had finished her master's degree and was pursuing her Ph.D., but her family wanted her married. In her culture women usually married young. She was beginning to feel the pressure from her family and her biological clock was alarming.

As a result, she began to cruise the club scene with a friend but never felt comfortable in that space. She would comment to me that her friend would walk in and all the men in the club would line up at her feet. I told her about the quantity vs. quality rule. Her friend had many relationships that would start with a bang and fizzle out quickly, but just because her options were plentiful didn't mean that they were quality options. My friend had a much different agenda, her desire was marriage and happily ever after. She needed a different kind of man than what her friend would normally date. I cautioned her to look for the quality rather than quantity.

A person that's looking for a long-term healthy mutually respectful relationship will have a much different agenda and persona than someone who frequents the clubs every night to find a new conquest. She understood the concept, but saw the statistics about women over thirty never being married. She went into a panic and succumbed to

127

the pressure placed upon her by her family and her biological clock. Instead of staying true to herself, her goals and ambition, she became obsessed with getting married. Internet dating, speed dating, and singles groups at various churches and meet-up groups became her priority. She chose to go into what I call "desperate girl zone".

It didn't take long for her to meet someone. He was a very nice guy, but they didn't have the same goals. He was an easily content person, not particularly ambitious, just an average all around good guy, who wanted to be a family man. He loved her and even passed the parent test. He was a sincere person with a heart of gold. I believe she loved him, but was not in love with him.

For a while the relationship was great. They hit the major relationship milestones and married a year after they met. She was pregnant two years later and a second child was born three years later. He was an excellent father who took over most of the parenting roles and gave her the time and support to finish her degree plan and meet her professional goals.

He was a good decent guy that she practically destroyed when she admitted to herself that she wasn't happy and had never really loved him. She liked and respected him but didn't feel passion for him and after seven years of marriage and two babies into the relationship, she was miserable. It wasn't long before she began to resent him because she felt trapped and tied to a life and a lifestyle that she didn't want.

She found solace in the arms of her co-worker that she had been interested in for years. He was recently divorced and she was sad, lonely and very depressed. It was not long before a relationship started. Her husband discovered the relationship and was crushed, her parents were mortified and she was madly in love. A bitter divorce ensued. The custody battle for their children was venomous to say the least. She practically destroyed her husband and two precious babies were in the middle of it all. Her family rallied around her husband and she was a pitiful, emotional mess. Her decisions ended her marriage and the life that she tried to build with the man she had always loved was strained at best. She left a wreckage that affected everyone she loved.

She had allowed some arbitrary time-line and the desires of her family to affect her marriage decisions.

If you are feeling similar pressure, please bear in mind that the people you meet are real people with feelings and emotions. If you aren't sincere, please don't use them as seat fillers until the one you really want comes along. If your heart isn't completely there, please take some time out and think it over very carefully. Think about the lives you may leave in ruins if you don't stand for the quality of love that you deserve. It's unfair and there could be serious consequences as a result. Try to avoid seat fillers, unless full disclosure has been made and both parties know what to expect.

The moral of the story is to take your time and find the right person for you. Don't adhere to anyone else's timetable. It's your life hold out for a quality love.

In case the journey to the right coupling takes one, two or maybe even five years, wait for the quality that you deserve. The question of quality over quantity will always exist. I hope you take the time and answer the question and realize who you are, what you want and what it means to be in mad and passionate love with someone who also loves you madly and passionately.

Your Assignment for today is to decide how you will define quality.

DAY 36
Take a Deep Breathe
Learning in Action

There have been many topics covered in *Break-up Breakthrough* and if you've used the program the way it was designed to be used, you've learned a lot about yourself, your wants, needs and your Deal Breakers. Now it's time to put the learning into action.

You should have a plan on how these lessons will be applied, how to use your brain and your heart to choose that person that will compliment you and walk life's journey with you. Love is always about the heart, but you have to use your head sometimes and not let your emotions run rampant and rule over your good senses.

Sometimes strong emotions can lead you to places that you will later regret. You have to learn to balance your emotions with all logical arguments, for or against a relationship. You have to be selective in order to find an enduring love rather than an emotional train wreck. It takes knowing where you are and where you want to go, to arrive at your destination.

You don't want to drag a partner with you, screaming and hollering all the way. You want someone who will go willingly and be able to make the necessary changes to have a successful relationship that's fulfilling and nurturing. Sometimes, you have to kiss a few frogs and learn to appreciate spinach to get to that point. Other times you will you have to simply change your way of thinking and communicating.

It's not always the other person that's the problem. Sometimes it's your expectations, your lack of communication or your attempt to fix previous relationships with parents or past lovers. So take a deep breath and commit yourself to looking for the love you want and need. Not from a space of desperation with your biological clock ticking, but from the space of living your best life, making your dreams true and creating a space for the possibility of meeting the person that you were created for. Until that day comes, be the love you deserve.

The key to being successful is to relax into the process of healing and to keep evolving into a better you. If you are frantic about your biological clock or some other time restraint that you've developed, the process will be more difficult to navigate because you will feel that you're behind and that you should be at some point other than where you are. You may feel that you've wasted too many years with this person or that person. But the truth of the matter is, the past is the past, the future is not yet and we have to live and enjoy today. You have to accept that nothing that has been done, can be undone. We all have to deal with where we are right now.

You can't spend too much time wishing and reminiscing; it's pointless and fruitless. You have to take a deep breath, relax and know that from this point on it can be and will be different. Even though from the exterior you see sameness, your awareness has created a new, improved and better you, that some great man/woman is searching for. Please don't disappoint them by giving up too soon.

Take a deep breath and go out into the world in all the glory and splendor that's YOU! Know that you are enough. You are now aware of your past patterns and you have the tools to make better decisions. Your intentions have been set, your tools have been sharpened and you have learned your lessons. Now you will attract a different kind of partner because you are different. And if by chance you attract someone that feels too familiar, you don't have to keep him/her. You can bless that person and send them into the universe for someone who will be accepting and appreciative of who they are. Don't dwell on the past, use it only as a reminder to make better decisions.

Remember the first day of school, when you really didn't want to go? You didn't know who you would meet, what type of environment you would have to experience or exist in, what the people in that environment would think of you, or what you would think of them? You were forced to leave your familiar environment for a new place, unknown and scary.

131

This process will be similar. You have made it through the first day of school, there were a few bumps in the road, and a few people who were difficult to deal with and some may not have been to your particular liking. Others were fun to play with, some cried all day, some were smart, others not so much, but you survived and thrived. You will experience the same kind of challenges and you will succeed, just like you did in first grade.

You probably made some lifelong friends and have fun memories that you can look back on and laugh. You probably met some people that if you didn't see them again, you'd not be terribly distraught. As you experience this journey to a loving relationship, you'll meet some people that you'll wonder how you ever made it this far without knowing, you'll meet some people that will not meet your fancy and others that will make you laugh. Finally, you will meet some lifelong friends and a love that will last forever. The most important thing to do is to get out there.

Your assignment for today is to plan three outings that you will participate in that will broaden your horizons and place you in a position to meet new and fun people.

132

DAY 37
Lessons Learned

"Some of the things I know, I know only because older women have told me their secrets. I have lived and am living long so that I can tell my secrets to young women. That is the reason we women go on improving."

-Maya Angelou

I found this quote several years ago in a greeting card, and it exemplifies what I'd like my legacy to be; to share with other women/men so they can minimize their suffering from heartaches and heartbreaks and find their way to a breakthrough.

At this point, I'd like to ask you to do the same. During the course of these thirty-seven days, I hope and pray that you have learned some lessons that have been meaningful to you that may also be powerful light bulb moments for others.

Today, I hope that you will take the time to stop and think about the process, the exercises, the insights, the openings in your Spirit and the cracks in your armor, and share the lessons you have learned. Think carefully, what did you learn about you, about relationships, about your wants and needs? Take the time to write these lessons down so that you can go back to them easily and remind yourself when your days become difficult and you're lonely and thinking that you may never find the love of your life. Then go to my website and share a lesson, share an insight that might make another person's journey easier. Share your failures and your successes. The cost you paid in relationships and the insights you've had. Please share:

- What questions should you ask yourself before getting into another relationship?
- What did your past relationships have in common?
- What do you know now that you wish you had known then?

133

- How have you picked up the pieces?
- What was the hardest part for you?
- Did it get easier?
- What advice would you give?
- Will you share these insights and tell your secrets so we all can go on improving?

Your Assignment for today is to find someone in your circle that might need a word of encouragement and share your story. Share your lessons and insights. Help us get better, be the valuable piece of the puzzle that we need to be complete.

LAST THINGS
R U OK?

To endure a divorce or break-up can be devastating and very painful. It can leave you physically and emotionally broken and in some extreme cases it can take many years to repair the damage. It's not something that you can take a deep breath and instantly overcome. So the question is, are you okay? Only you can answer that question. If the answer is yes, I'm so very happy for you. If you are getting there but you know it will take awhile and you have decided to take some time to rediscover your real self, then I hope and pray that you've found something in these pages that will help you get back to yourself and to the love that you desire and deserve.

If you answered "no", and you know you're not okay, your pain is still too much for you, please seek some professional help. It's always okay to ask for help and it's necessary sometimes to have someone that you can lean on until you're stronger. Evaluate your circumstances and do what is best for you. It's imperative that you get the help you need. Please seek some professional help in your area or contact me for one-on-one work.

If by chance you answered, "no, but," because you are not okay, but you don't feel like you need professional help but rather a little more clarification from me to help develop a plan specifically for you. Please feel free to contact me.

Until I hear from you again, Blessings and "GOOD LOVE" to you.

135

35110993R00083

Made in the USA
Middletown, DE
19 September 2016